Cracking the Success Code
The Best Business Lesson I Have Ever Learned
H7 Network Members

Infinite Impressions Publishing

Infinite Impressions Publishing

Book Cover by David Vasudevan

Edited by Lori Karpman and Angel Hicks

Published by Infinite Impressions Publishing

1st edition 2025

Contents

Dedication written by the Authors:

Chapter 1 written by Lori Karpman

To my son and greatest fan, Evan, whose support has been the cornerstone of my journey. Your love and encouragement has made all my accomplishments possible. Love you to the moon and back.

Chapter 2 written by Clay Hicks

My wife is my muse. She knows this story well but had I not gone through all the fires, I would have never met my muse. She makes all things in my life better.

Chapter 4 written by Donna Grande

To my mother, Grace Grande, you taught me that gratitude isn't just a feeling – it's a way of life. To my husband, Scott Goroski– thank you for being my steady rock. Forever grateful. Always inspired.

Chapter 6 written by Dan Casanta

To my wife, Jane- my unwavering compass, whose support, belief, and love illuminate every step of my journey.

Chapter 8 written by Angel Hicks

I dedicate my chapter to my husband Clay who has stuck by me no matter how many times I've evolved into someone new.

Chapter 10 written by Coach Hess

I dedicate my chapter to Earvin "Magic" Johnson, Jr. who has been an inspiration and leader in transforming many from the court to boardroom.

Introduction

By Lori Karpman

In the ever-evolving landscape of business, adaptability is not just a virtue; it's a necessity. This anthology, "The Best Business Lesson I Ever Learned," brings together a diverse array of experiences from successful entrepreneurs, each sharing their most impactful insights. As the curator of this project, I've witnessed firsthand the transformative power of collaborative storytelling.

The Anthology Advantage

Contributing to an anthology book is a smart strategy for professionals aiming to boost their brand and authority. I have participated in three Amazon bestselling anthology projects. The credibility and exposure gained from this approach is invaluable. Anthologies allow you to showcase your expertise alongside other industry leaders, expanding your reach and audience diversity beyond what a solo author could achieve. It provides a platform, network, and credibility stamp, marking you as an Amazon bestselling author—a title that signifies your expertise and voice on a matter. Anthologies are also cost-effective and accessible, offering a simpler alternative to writing a full-length book, which requires significant time, effort, and money. By sharing your unique insights, you establish yourself as a thought leader, making anthologies an efficient and democratic way to step into authorship and gain recognition.

I created *The Best Business Lesson I Ever Learned* as an anthology book to give authors—each an expert in their respective field—a powerful platform to showcase their credibility and share the wisdom they've gained through real-world experience. The idea stemmed from a simple truth: every professional, no matter their industry, has faced pivotal moments that shaped their success. By curating these stories into one collection, I wanted to offer a space where contributors could elevate their authority, connect with a broader audience, and inspire others through lessons that only come from lived experience.

I chose the topic "The Best Business Lesson I Ever Learned" because it's universal yet deeply personal. Business is a vast landscape, and the lessons that stick with us often transcend industries, speaking to challenges, triumphs, and growth we all encounter. Each contributor brings their unique perspective, distilled into a single, impactful lesson from their career—whether it's about leadership, resilience, innovation, or navigating failure. For readers, the point is connection and application: you'll see yourself in one or more of these stories, finding parallels to your own journey. This anthology isn't just a showcase of expertise; it's a toolkit of actionable takeaways that can spark new ideas, refine your strategies, or simply remind you that you're not alone in the hurdles you face.

The contributors, all seasoned experts, pour their authentic experiences into this book, making it a rich tapestry of knowledge and inspiration. As a reader, you'll not only gain insights to apply in your own life or career but also witness the power of shared storytelling. I invite you to share *The Best Business Lesson I Ever Learned* with your colleagues, friends, and network. The more people who engage with it, the greater the possibilities—for the contributors, whose voices amplify with every share, and for readers like you, who can spark conversations, build connections, and uncover new opportunities through these lessons. Together, we can turn this anthology into a movement of growth and impact.

I'd be remiss if I did not mention my partner in crime, Angel Hicks. Working with Angel Hicks has been an absolute joy! She is the consummate professional—organized, insightful, and deeply committed to excellence. As a brilliant publisher, she brings a perfect blend of creativity and expertise to every project, making the entire process seamless and rewarding. What truly sets Angel apart is her ability to make work feel like fun, turning collaboration into an inspiring and enjoyable experience.

Happy Reading to you All.

Lori Karpman

H7 Market Area Director

Chapter 1

The Power of Pivoting

Lori Karpman

My Journey: A Testament to Adaptability

From a young age, I recognized the importance of continuous learning and professional development. Education has been the cornerstone of my career evolution, empowering me to seize new opportunities and expand my skill set.

Throughout my professional journey, I have taken on multiple roles: attorney, management consultant,

> 66
> Pivoting isn't a sign of failure—it's a mark of resilience."
> — Reid Hoffman (co-founder of LinkedIn)
> 99

restaurant franchise creator and chain owner, executive recruiter, sales trainer, Kolbe consultant, and Story Brand trained professional copywriter. Each role has provided me with a new perspective and additional services to offer my clients.

My own professional journey is a testament to the power of pivoting. My career has been a series of strategic shifts, each building upon the last to create a unique skill set that spans multiple industries and disciplines.

Over the years, I've worn many hats. Each role has been a chapter in a winding, evolving story of adaptation and reinvention. But if I had to boil it all down to one defining truth, the best business lesson I ever learned is this: the importance of being able to pivot when the life or the business environment changes.

I've made continuing education a staple in my life, both personal and professional, not just because I love to learn, but because I've seen firsthand how quickly the world can shift beneath your feet. Over the course of my career, I've transitioned through multiple industries and professions, each one building on the last, each one teaching me how to adapt to new challenges and seize new opportunities. My ability to pivot hasn't just been a survival skill—it's been the key to thriving in an ever-changing landscape.

An Early Start

My passion for writing began at the age of nine when I created a school newspaper in fourth grade. By fifth grade, I had become the Editor, leading a team of student reporters covering everything from sports to weather to school events—a glimpse of what was to come. Throughout high school, my essays earned prestigious awards. Over the years, I have published more than 250 articles, contributed to three anthology books, and achieved Amazon bestselling author status three times. Recently my company, The Copy Lab garnered an award for Best Innovation in Digital Marketing, an achievement I am extremely grateful for as I was nominated by a 3rd party.

From Business School to Law School

My entrepreneurial spirit took root early. At just eleven years old, I managed a paper route, and soon after, I began working in my father's jewelry wholesale business. By 19, I had earned my place as a senior executive—not a title simply handed to me. When my father suffered a heart attack, I stepped up to run the business at 20, ensuring its continued success until he was able to return. This was a struggle as I was in university at the time. But I had to step up. That experience provided invaluable lessons about the business world—insights that would serve me well throughout my career.

Despite running the business full time, I graduated McGill University Suma Cum Laude and earned a Bachelor of Commerce in Marketing and Management Information Systems. Both disciplines would be important and impactful for my future career as an entrepreneur and business owner.

One of the things I realize quickly is that my logic skills are great with words, but not so much with numbers. Finance was out for me, but law, where I could spend my day writing and speaking, was calling my name.

From Law to Hospitality

My legal career began in the structured world of tax law in a private law firm, where precision and attention to detail were paramount. After 7 years of practicing private law I decided it was time for a change. I was offered the position of the VP of Legal Affairs and HR for a multi-million dollar hospitality company that owned and operated 3 chains of restaurants, all within the franchise industry. During my 10 year tenure I gained invaluable insights into the franchise model and the intricacies of managing multiple brands. I learned about legalities, financing, operations, development, sales and marketing of franchises.

This experience laid the groundwork for my next venture: co-founding and franchising my own chain of wildly successful restaurants. With a multitude of awards behind it, my brand immediately drew the attention of restaurateurs nationwide. After having successfully developed 21 locations, I was approached by a US based, restaurant development company looking to buy the rights to my brand for the USA. I sold the entire business and stepped into a moment of uncertainty. I don't deal with uncertainty well so this was a very emotional time. I'd spent years building something from the ground up, and now it was gone. What came next? I didn't have a clear answer, so I pivoted again—this time into executive recruiting within the hospitality industry.

Another Pivot Point to Executive Recruiting

The sale of my restaurant chain marked a critical juncture in my career. Faced with the question of "what do I do now that I am grown up?", I made a decision that would come to define my professional philosophy: I pivoted. Drawing on my restaurant industry connections and knowledge, I transitioned into executive recruiting for the hospitality sector.

This two-year stint as a recruiter was more than just a job; it was a strategic move that allowed me to maintain and expand my network while I plotted my next big move. It was during this time that I recognized the value of my unique blend of legal expertise and practical business experience in the franchise world.

But then it all came crashing down.

Then Life Happened....and happened... and happened...

In my relentless pursuit to grow my restaurant chain, I drove myself beyond my limits, sacrificing my health until my body could no longer keep pace. The result was a diagnosis of Crohn's Disease—a chronic, debilitating condition that I continue to manage daily with unwavering determination. After two years away from work, my marriage dissolved, leaving me a single mother to two young children, ages 7 and 11 and no income. Like many women, I grappled with the persistent doubt that I wasn't measuring up—neither as a professional nor as a mother—amid a struggle that tested every ounce of my resolve. Yet life had more challenges in store: over the next four years, I lost both of my parents, my greatest sources of inspiration and support, taken far too early. Balancing their care in their final days with the demands of raising my children left little space for my career, and the financial strain became insurmountable. Ultimately, I chose bankruptcy—not as a mark of defeat, but as a deliberate step toward liberation. While society often casts it as humiliation, I saw it as a pragmatic reset, a tool designed for those, like me, facing debts too vast to conquer in one lifetime. It was a decision rooted in clarity and strength, offering me the chance to rebuild on my own terms.

The Birth of Lori Karpman & Company

After my divorce I had to earn my own income. Now a single mother of 2 I had to find a way to earn a living. I knew that I had to work from home so that I could continue to parent the way I wanted to. Armed with a comprehensive understanding of the franchise industry, I established Lori Karpman & Company, a full-service franchise development firm in 2003. This venture was the culmination of my years of varied experience in the franchise world, allowing me to offer clients a holistic approach to franchising.

Having been a franchisor twice, a master franchisee, an attorney, and a franchise consultant allowed me to offer a complete suite of turnkey solutions for brands wanting to expand via the franchise or license model. To this day, the multi-award Lori Karpman & Company is the only "one -stop shop" for franchised or licensed business development.

As a management consultant, I understood the importance of continuous education and skill development. Over the years, I've acquired a diverse array of credentials, each chosen to complement and enhance my service offerings. This commitment to learning has enabled me to provide turn-key solutions for businesses looking to franchise, addressing every aspect from legal considerations to operational best practices.

The Evolution Continues, From Lawyer to Copywriter

My professional evolution didn't stop there. Recognizing the power of effective communication in business, I tapped into my lifelong love of writing—the very passion that had initially drawn me to the practice of law. This led to the creation of my latest venture, "The Copy Lab," where I apply my persuasive writing skills honed in my legal practice to the world of creative content.

Becoming Story Brand trained, a writing certification created by Donald Miller, was a natural progression, allowing me to merge my legal background with modern marketing techniques. This latest pivot has enabled me to offer clients not just legal and business expertise, but also compelling narrative strategies to enhance their brand messaging. I create content that converts.

My legal background has also significantly shaped my copywriting approach, combining legal precision with marketing creativity. Key skills from my legal career - attention to detail, research proficiency, and ethical awareness - enhance my copywriting. I balance technical accuracy with accessibility, structure complex information clearly, and apply persuasive techniques learned in law. Adapting from formal legal writing to a more engaging, conversational style, I create content that is both legally sound and appealing to diverse audiences. My copy effectively bridging the legal and marketing worlds and increasing sales conversions. The transition has allowed me to combine the precision of legal writing with the creativity and accessibility required in marketing communications.

The Lesson: Embrace Change and Never Stop Learning

The most valuable business lesson I've learned throughout my multifaceted career is the critical importance of being able to pivot when life or the business environment changes. This adaptability, coupled with a commitment to continuous learning, has been the cornerstone of my success.

In today's rapidly changing business landscape, the ability to recognize shifts in the market and adjust your strategy accordingly is invaluable. My journey from tax attorney to VP Legal Affairs, to restauranteur to recruiter to franchise expert to copywriter, illustrates that career paths are rarely linear. Each role I've taken on, each new skill I've acquired, has added another layer to my professional toolkit.

Continuous education and the mindset that goes with it, has been a staple in my life, allowing me to stay ahead of industry trends and offer innovative solutions to my clients. Whether it's obtaining new certifications, learning cutting-edge marketing techniques, or simply staying informed about changes in the business world, this commitment to learning has been crucial in maintaining my competitive edge.

The Power of Diverse Experience

My varied career path has given me a unique perspective on business challenges. This diversity of experience allows me to approach problems from multiple angles, often finding solutions that others might overlook.

For instance, my legal background provides a solid foundation for understanding the regulatory aspects of franchising, while my experience as a franchise owner offers practical insights into day-to-day operations. My time in executive recruitment honed my ability to identify top talent, a crucial skill for any growing business. And now, with my copywriting expertise, I can help businesses not just establish themselves, but also effectively communicate their value to potential customers thereby increasing sales and profit. By adapting my legal writing skills—once used to construct airtight arguments in court—to create compelling brand narratives, I've been able to help businesses connect with their audience in meaningful ways. This pivot not only expanded my service offerings but also allowed me to stay relevant in an increasingly digital business environment.

The Anthology: A Culmination of Lessons Learned

Participating in this anthology is, in itself, a strategic pivot. It's an opportunity to share my expertise with a wider audience, to learn from the experiences of others, and to be part of a collective effort that elevates all contributors. Just as I've pivoted throughout my career to stay relevant and valuable to my clients, this anthology represents a pivot in how I think about business education and personal branding.

Conclusion: The Journey Continues

As I reflect on the best business lesson I've ever learned—the importance of pivoting and continuous learning—I'm reminded that this lesson is never truly finished. Life and in particular, the business world will continue to evolve, and with it, so must we.

In the end, the most successful businesses and professionals are not those who resist change, but those who anticipate it, embrace it, and use it as a catalyst for growth. As you read through the chapters of this book, I encourage you to consider your own pivotal moments and the lessons they've taught you. And remember, in life and in the world of business, the learning never stops, and the next big pivot might be just around the corner.

***

Author Bio:

Lori Karpman is a distinguished business consultant, franchise expert, professional speaker and award winning copywriter with over 30 years of diverse experience in corporate and non-profit sectors.

She holds a Bachelor of Commerce degree, specializing in Marketing and Management Information Systems, as well as degrees in Civil and Common Law, all from McGill University in Montreal.

As the founder and CEO of the multi-award-winning firm, Lori Karpman & Company, Lori offers comprehensive business development services, including strategic growth planning, brand architecture, franchising and licensing, and executive coaching. Her firm is renowned for its vert holistic approach, providing clients with a one-stop shop for all their business development needs.

As the Chief Creative Officer of The Copy Lab, Lori creates compelling content for businesses that convert prospects to clients.

Lori's expertise in franchising is unparalleled. She has firsthand experience as both a franchisor and franchisee, having served as the Master Franchisee of Pizza Hut for Quebec and as President of her own franchised brand, Zyng Noodlery, which she successfully sold to a U.S. development group. Her deep understanding of the legal and practical aspects of franchising has made her a sought-after consultant in the industry.

Beyond her consulting work, Lori is a prolific writer and an engaging public speaker. She shares her insights on business growth, leadership, and personal development, aiming to inspire and empower her audiences. Her personal journey, including overcoming health challenges, adds depth to her presentations, leaving listeners motivated and equipped with actionable strategies.

Lori's dedication and excellence have been recognized with numerous accolades, including being named Business Management Consultant of the Year and receiving the Outstanding Management Consultancy Firm award. Her firm has also been honored as the Best Franchising Consultancy and listed among the Top 25 Innovative Companies to Watch. Most recently The Copy Lab was awarded the honor of being "Innovative Digital Marketing" award.

In addition to her professional pursuits, Lori is committed to giving back to the community through extensive non-profit and Board of Directors work. Her multifaceted career and unwavering commitment to excellence make her a leading figure in business consulting, franchising and content creation.

Chapter 2

Lone Wolf Finds His Pack

Clay Hicks

Part One: The Lone Wolf's Downfall

    In my early twenties I was a relentless hustler, navigating the crazy waters of the real estate investment industry. Through my chase of success, I had inadvertently created a solitary endeavor. Until a few years later, when it all came crashing down on me the year I turned 26. I found myself divorced and a newly single father of two young girls with full custody. Thrust into the dual role of entrepreneur and single fatherhood with sole custody, the challenges were mounting, and the hustle was relentless.

    At this stage, life had stripped away the comforts and securities I once knew. Financial strains and personal hardships became my new normal,

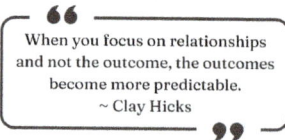

> **66**
> When you focus on relationships and not the outcome, the outcomes become more predictable.
> ~ Clay Hicks
> **99**

and my entrepreneurial spirit—though undeterred—wrestled with the stark realities of going it alone. The independence I clung to came with its own set of pitfalls. I operated like a lone wolf in a world that demanded collaboration. My struggle was not just against competitors but against the tendency to isolate myself professionally. I knew branching out to collaborate with others was what was best for me but my pride and ego were too big for me to take that leap. That was quickly about to change.

The breaking point came as I juggled real estate deals, the pressures of raising kids, and grasping for stability in a sea of uncertainty. I discovered two potential partners in the industry, professionals who were flipping houses, much like I was. They offered the promise of collaboration, yet my instincts inclined toward autonomy. Initially, our partnership felt promising, a chance to form a pack and leverage our collective strengths. However, my own insecurities and pride became hindrances—I was torn between the comfort of independence and the benefits of collaboration.

With the pressure mounting, an incident drove the lesson home. I faced a significant financial shortfall and asked a partner for a loan to cover my rent. His response was candid: "You need to prove yourself; close this deal with us first." This challenge forced me into action. I pursued the sale with determination, yet I leaned heavily on potential buyers who, I had hoped, would help clinch the deal. In a surprising turn of fate, leveraging these relationships enabled the sale, validating my partner's trust and securing my financial footing. And my rent was paid.

This experience illuminated my path forward—collaboration wasn't just beneficial; it was essential. Circumstances have shown me that success isn't born from isolation but from weaving into the fabric of a community. The once proud lone wolf began to see the value of mingling with the pack.

Part Two: Shared Burdens Lead to Shared Success

The second pivotal lesson I encountered on my journey was both practical and transformative: the understanding that sharing our burdens leads to shared success. This insight not only redefined my perception of achievement but also marked a profound turning point in how I approached both life and business during one of the most challenging times of my life. After my mom had passed away in October of 2007, I found myself standing at a crossroads.

Her passing, merely months after closing a crucial house deal, left a void that solitude could never fill. As the reality of my new responsibilities settled in, I realized that I had to step up not only for my daughters but also for my Pops, who now relied on me more than ever. With no siblings to share this burden, it was a period of reflection and re-evaluation.

In those early days of mourning, I felt my life lacked direction and purpose. The loneliness was palpable, amplifying the grief and uncertainty of my circumstances. I turned towards a higher power, seeking solace and clarity. Mornings spent in meditation with the Lord became a cornerstone of my daily routine. These quiet moments offered me peace and transformed my anxiety into a sense of serenity, setting the stage for a renewed outlook on life.

As I ventured into the world of professional networking, my need for trusted relationships became increasingly apparent. Following the closure of a networking group to which I belonged, I embarked on a journey to find a new home for my goals. Many groups I visited felt restrictive, had too many rules and requirements that clashed with the entrepreneurial freedom I had gotten used to. The chambers I visited didn't offer the sense of belonging I needed, leading to increased frustration.

Then came a pivotal moment of realization: "There must be others like me who long for meaningful relationships without the constraints of rigid rules." It was at this moment that I trusted my instincts and asked a trusted acquaintance if he thought I could create such a space. Encouraged by his support and belief in my vision, I took a leap of faith. With his help, I assembled a group of four professionals who would become the founding members of what was initially called Tri-State Business Network, which later evolved into *H7 Network*.

Despite financial challenges, I used a portion of the small inheritance my mother left to get the network off the ground. The initial investment of $200, coupled with the unwavering support of my new-found allies, enabled us to begin our journey. Together, we kicked things into gear, growing the network by 60 members in our first year, followed by a year of doubling in size. My trusted relationships with these original members laid a foundation for success and growth, allowing us to create something truly remarkable.

Working with others introduced me to a wealth of diverse perspectives that enriched my own. The unique insights each partner brought to the table sparked a flood of new ideas and approaches. These collaborative efforts resulted in innovative solutions I could never have conceived on my own, illustrating the transformative power of shared perspectives. It demonstrated that by lifting one another up, we could ascend to greater heights collectively rather than individually.

A significant revelation during this journey was the concept of shared risk—initially daunting, yet eventually invaluable. Distributing responsibilities and potential setbacks across a network of professionals made challenges more manageable. What once felt like insurmountable obstacles became opportunities for growth, transformed through the combined strength and resilience of a supportive team.

In embracing collaboration, I feared my role might diminish. But instead, it amplified our collective achievements, enhancing our overall capacity. This dynamic nature of teamwork opened doors that were once inaccessible to a lone operator, underscoring the profound impact of our collaborative effort.

The shift from individual pursuits to communal endeavors was both liberating and inspiring. No longer confined by my limitations, collaboration taught me to leverage the strengths and skills of those around me, forming a collage of diverse talents and expertise. This change prompted a recalibration of my approach to business and life, emphasizing the crucial value of teamwork and community.

Prioritizing collective effort unlocked dimensions of success that extended beyond traditional measures. The benefits of partnership transcended monetary gain, fostering a sense of community and fulfillment that enriched both my personal and professional life. Together, we celebrated victories and navigated setbacks, learning and growing through shared experiences.

The realization that shared burdens equate to shared success redefined my perception of achievement. It taught me that embracing the power of collaboration unveils endless possibilities, allowing me to reach unprecedented potentials through a united, collective spirit. This lesson, etched into my evolution as an entrepreneur, emphasizes the essence of working together and serves as a reminder that the true measure of success lies not in individual accolades, but in the shared journeys that shape us. With the Lord guiding my steps and community support by my side, I embraced an approach where endless possibilities could unfold, transcending the limitations of a solitary existence.

Part Three: Integrating Wisdom into Practice

Reflecting on the journey from solitary endeavors to building the H7 Network, the transformative power of collaboration and shared vision has been undeniably profound. The early seeds, sown with intention and nurtured through partnerships, blossomed into something far greater than I could have achieved alone. By integrating wisdom into practice, embracing inclusion, and fostering a shared vision, I transitioned from a solitary entrepreneur to a community-driven leader.

Throughout this journey, a fundamental truth became evident: "When you focus on relationships and not the outcomes, the outcomes become more predictable." It's this focus on nurturing genuine trusted relationships that has consistently paved the path to success, demonstrating time and again that relationships are the cornerstone of any thriving business model.

This is where my company's tenet "Connect, Serve, Ask ^{TM}" came into play. The philosophy of *Connect, Serve, and Ask*^{TM} was born not from a textbook or a business plan, but from a deeply personal and transformative journey that began on August 1st, 2014. At the time, I had no idea that a simple commitment to showing up, meeting people one-on-one, and building relationships would fundamentally change my life—and eventually become a guiding framework that would serve others too.

In the early days, I was simply trying to build something meaningful. I didn't have a name for it, nor did I fully understand what I was creating. But I *did* know this: people matter. And relationships matter more than we often give them credit for. So I kept showing up, over and over again.

It wasn't until I reached 2,500 one-to-one conversations that I finally embraced the power of the *Ask*. Up until then, I was committed to giving—listening, helping, connecting—but I hesitated when it came to receiving or inviting others to support my own journey. That "aha" moment, which arrived around January 2018, cracked something open in me. It revealed the truth that *asking* is not selfish—it's an essential part of healthy, reciprocal relationships. When done with integrity and intention, the *Ask* becomes an invitation into something bigger than ourselves.

By August of that year, the philosophy began to take shape. I identified the first two elements—*Connect* and *Serve*—as foundational, calling them "infinite relationships" and "adding value to others." They felt natural, like breathing. But once *Ask* was added to the framework, everything came into alignment. The pieces clicked. The purpose behind my years of intentional relationship-building became clear.

But clarity doesn't always mean completion. It took another 500 one-to-ones—bringing the total to 3,000—to refine the method into something repeatable, something that could be taught and passed on. Each conversation became a thread in the fabric of something bigger than me. And since that day, I've applied the *Connect, Serve, and Ask™* approach more than 5,700 times. Every interaction has reinforced this belief: *there are no coincidences.* People come into our lives for a reason, and when we show up with openness, generosity, and courage, we build trust that transcends transactions.

Along this path, I discovered not only a powerful methodology—but also my purpose.

They say the two most important days in a person's life are the day they're born and the day they discover why. For me, the "why" was revealed in the quiet spaces between conversations, in the uplifted faces of others when they felt truly seen, heard, and supported. My purpose is to lift others, nurture their potential, and unite them in meaningful connection. And above all, to recognize that no success is ever mine alone. Everything I have built, every milestone reached, is the result of *we*, not *me*.

This is more than a philosophy. It's a way of living.

Connect, Serve, and Ask™ is not just about networking or growing a business—it's about transforming the way we build relationships. It's about planting seeds of trust, watering them with generosity, and allowing them to grow through mutual support and purposeful action. It's about creating a ripple effect of empowerment and connection that reaches far beyond our own circles.

For those embarking on similar paths, I encourage you to pause and reflect on your current journey. Consider the relationships that surround you—identify those potential partners and collaborators who share your vision or possess skills that complement your own. It is through these meaningful connections that the most unpredictable outcomes can become a reality. Approaching these relationships with openness, humility, and a willingness to learn will foster not just growth, but a personal and professional fulfillment that transcends traditional measures of success.

As I stand today, an entrepreneur deeply fulfilled by the robust fruits of collaboration, I wish you a journey enriched by your own discoveries and connections. May you find your own pack, your community of support and inspiration, and may the path you tread together reveal possibilities beyond your imagination. Remember, while the journey may seem solitary at times, immense opportunities unfold when walked with the right people by your side.

To all the lone wolves out there, poised on the brink of reimagining their journey—embrace the power of collaboration, and let it guide you to a future where possibilities are limitless. Here's to your success and the shared journeys that will undoubtedly shape your path. Blessings to you on your adventure, and may the relationships you build lead to outcomes as remarkable as the journey itself.

***

Author Bio:

Clay Hicks, an innovator and entrepreneur with a passion for fostering professional relationships, stands as a transformative force in the business world.

As the visionary behind the H7 Network, founded in 2008, Clay developed the first ever Word-of-Mouth Marketing platform that focuses solely on Connect, Serve, and Ask ©. His purpose in life is to value others, lifting them up, developing and uniting them, and taking no credit for their success. Driven by this mission, Clay empowers the underrepresented—the dreamers, doers, and relentless entrepreneurs striving to rewrite their destinies alongside professionals supporting their word-of-mouth marketing efforts.

Under Clay's visionary leadership, the H7 Network thrives as a pioneering B2B networking ecosystem, creating environments where professionals connect deeply. His commitment extends beyond geographical boundaries, with H7 establishing a strong presence across 48 states and reaching 22 countries, including Canada, Israel, Hungary, Egypt, and England. The H7 Network is more than just a platform; it's a movement and a testament to Clay's belief that success is a shared journey. By nurturing relationships rooted in trust and mutual growth, Clay ensures the network continues its impressive global expansion, empowering individuals to break barriers, inspire change, and reshape their futures with the unyielding support of a community that believes in the power of word-of-mouth connections.

Chapter 3

Grace in Every Step

Bill Walters

I t's pretty ironic when one step feels like a thousand miles. For as long as I can remember, my parents made it clear that education would always be a priority. It wasn't a matter of if I would go to college but when. In our household, the expectation wasn't just that I would attend school but that I would excel—get good grades, do my best, and graduate.

There was never any question about my path; it was a matter of following through. The pressure was

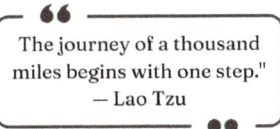

The journey of a thousand miles begins with one step."
— Lao Tzu

there, but it never felt overwhelming. My parents had this fantastic way of setting high expectations while ensuring I knew they had my back, no matter what. They taught me that success would come from hard work, discipline, and perseverance; that mindset stuck with me as I grew. Although, it wasn't always easy.

Life is rarely simple or predictable. When I was four, I was diagnosed with hip dysplasia. At the time, my doctors and parents explaining those words to me went over my head. As expected of any adolescent, I didn't understand that this condition would define my childhood. I don't remember much of the pain at first, but I do remember the disruption. I dislocated my hips several times as a child, sometimes by doing the simplest things—walking, bending over, or even just playing. Each time, I would be bedridden for weeks. It was torturous for a child who just wanted to run and play. My legs would grow weak, and I would have to relearn how to walk each time. The worst of it was the temporary paralysis. Just like the words "hip dysplasia," try explaining to a kid the technical term for why, some days, I couldn't move at all. There were moments when I could barely move. My parents would carry me to the bathroom and help me with everything. I couldn't go and get my food. I wasn't able to walk to the other room to grab something. I had a small service bell that I would ring to let my parents know I needed their help. I couldn't do anything without my parents or someone helping me. They'd get me everything I needed, but they could do nothing to take away the feeling of helplessness I often had. But in the middle of all this, something remarkable happened.

My mom, who had always been the emotional backbone of our family, knew that I needed more than just physical care. She couldn't let me become idle or feel isolated. So, she bought me an encyclopedia during my weeks of bed rest, and I lost myself in the pages. I devoured the books, soaking in the information. Back then, TV shows were limited and offered hardly any comfort. How many times can you possibly watch reruns of Gilligan's Island? The encyclopedia became my escape. I was learning things that seemed larger than life at a young age. The world of knowledge was vast, and I felt like I was a part of it, even if I was confined to my bed. I was physically a prisoner in my room, but in my mind, I was free.

I still yearned for a normal childhood. My mom made sure that I stayed involved at home. I had chores—nothing too strenuous, but enough to help around the house and feel like I was contributing. It wasn't just about checking things off a to-do list—it was about learning responsibility. It gave me a sense of routine and connected me to the world outside, even when I couldn't do everything my friends were doing.

Each time I was finally able to walk again, I faced the brutal reality of rehab. The physical challenges were grueling. Dr. Hoffman, the physician who had worked with me through my hip dislocations, was a calming presence during my recovery. He was one of those rare doctors who didn't just treat the condition; he treated the person. He told me repeatedly that if I followed his instructions, trusted him, and put in the work, I'd be just like all the other boys. It would just take a little longer for me. He made me feel like I could still be a normal kid. I didn't have to "catch up" with everyone else, and there wasn't a strict agenda to my progress. Each small victory was celebrated, and that helped me grow stronger.

The emotional support from my parents was equally as important as the physical rehabilitation. My mom stayed home to care for me, never leaving my side during those years of recovery. I was never alone. There was always someone there, a constant presence, to remind me that I was loved and cared for, even when my body wasn't cooperating. I had always been a curious kid, but those bedridden years made me realize how much I could achieve with my mind. I found solace in books, and my imagination grew. I learned to focus on setting achievable goals and then building on them. If I couldn't run or play sports yet, I could study harder, read more, and push myself in other ways.

By the time I reached high school, I had been "episode-free" for almost two years. Like most thirteen-year-old boys, I was getting stronger and wanted to enter this upcoming chapter of life with a new brand for myself, an image apart from being the class brainiac.

I participated in school plays (mainly as a background person) and attended parties. I wasn't going to let myself be a social outcast.

Crowded in the auditorium during freshman orientation, Coach Guillam stood up on the stage and made an inspiring speech about joining cross country. He talked about the greatness that came with being on a team and all of the glory that came with it. I was hooked.

Naturally, my parents were hesitant. My hips had hardly given me trouble since the pommel horse incident, but they were weary about me getting hurt. After much pleading and deliberation, they agreed to let me join the team. As expected, I had no idea what I was doing at first. I wasn't in great shape and could barely finish a three-mile practice. But, being the hard-headed and driven kid that I was, I stuck with it. I trained. I pushed through the pain and watched my times improve over the year. By the end of the season, I had shaved more than eight minutes from my initial time.

I became stronger, suddenly finding myself with boundless energy. In addition to track, I joined the tennis team, making varsity as a freshman. I was making progress and was finally a typical teenager. Even at the time, I knew winning wasn't everything. But I felt like a winner.

Looking back, I realize that the challenges I faced, from my physical limitations to my emotional struggles, are what shaped me into the person I am today. Without them, I wouldn't have developed the discipline, empathy, or resilience that defines me now. I wouldn't have learned to set small goals and build from there. Most importantly, I wouldn't have learned that true fulfillment comes from helping others. That's what gives my life meaning now—empowering others to achieve greatness by financially bettering themselves and their loved ones. It's a lesson I carry with me daily and am grateful for. I love sharing knowledge and experiences to benefit others, not myself. It's how I try to make the world around me a better place.

Beyond the Classroom

While I had focused most of my time in high school on being a regular teenager, college was an entirely different experience. I decided to attend Drexel University in Philadelphia to complete their 5-year Bachelor's program. My college education was anything but traditional. It was a period that felt, at times, like a test in and of itself. It was several years full of trials and tribulations, the lessons I learned not always stemming from lectures or textbooks.

As one might hope from the college experience, a few courses I took impacted me more than others. That said, I never thought a "Selling and Sales Management" class would teach me the grit I needed to survive and thrive. Can I be honest with you? When I first signed up for that class, I had no idea what I was walking into. I was eager to learn, but I was just another student. I thought this would be a typical class. But from the moment I stepped into the classroom, it was clear that this wouldn't be a standard college experience. I was about to get slapped in the face. Hard.

Professor Grassi was nothing like any other professor I had encountered. On the first day of class, she was stone-cold. She wasn't friendly or welcoming; she seemed downright hostile. I think she was trying to push people out. Her method was simple: If you weren't serious about learning, if you didn't have the grit to withstand some discomfort, you'd quit. And believe me, most people did. Within the first few weeks, nearly everyone had dropped out. By the end of the month, only about ten of us were left. And those ten students? We were the ones who could handle it.

Professor Grassi's strategy wasn't just about making us uncomfortable for the sake of it; she wanted to see who could withstand the pressure of rejection—the real-world stuff that anyone in sales faces daily. These are things you can't learn from a textbook. Her first exercise was brutal. She handed us an item from her purse with no real value and told us to sell it to her. The problem wasn't the item; it was the fact that she was purposefully cruel. She laughed at us, insulted our pitches, and threw every rejection in our faces. Terrible. She was like a mirror, showing us what we feared: failure. She wanted us to get used to rejection and learn to take it without breaking, to learn and get better from the experience (though it was hard to see then).

I remember thinking, "Why am I putting myself through this torture? What am I getting out of this class?" My friends and I would talk about how clinically insane we thought this all was. But the more she rejected me, the more I realized that it wasn't just about learning to sell a product—it was about learning to brave the storm and bounce back. By the end of the class, after weeks of rejection and humiliation, she finally gave us tips and actionable advice. But by then, we had already learned the most important lesson: how to keep going, even when you feel like you've failed, and learn from your failures to improve next time.

Despite feeling like I had gone to war instead of passing Selling and Sales Management, I still walked away with more than just a grade. I got a B+ in the class (one of the worst grades I ever received in my life), but that didn't reflect my lessons. I realized that resilience isn't just about overcoming failure—it's about embracing it and using it as a stepping stone toward something better. That's something I've carried with me throughout my entire career, but we'll get there.

Our final project was a game changer. We had to take a product to market and pitch to the entire class and other professors. The pressure of presenting something I had created in front of professionals was terrifying then, but it prepared me for what would come next in my career. It was a hands-on, real-world experience that gave me a taste of what it meant to be successful in the business world. That class wasn't just a requirement—it was the foundation of my career. Even today, I still utilize many strategies Professor Grassi taught me. I've built most of my career on lessons learned in that classroom. It wasn't until I returned to Drexel years later as a guest speaker that I finally saw Professor Grassi in a more human light. Realizing there had always been a method to her madness, she was preparing us to be successful in life. Doing well in her class meant you could make it anywhere.

Drexel gave me the tools I needed for life, even if the experience itself was less than glamorous. It wasn't about the degree or the grades-- I was prompted with challenges different from what I had already experienced in my young life. The real lessons came from the challenges: facing rejection, learning from mistakes, and pushing through setbacks and even embarrassment. Those experiences shaped how I would approach every stage of my career. But as I said, we'll get there.

A Chip Off The Old Block

Resiliency is a running theme in my family. If you want proof, just take a look at my daughter. Her health challenges would shock you. She was a joyful and bright child with the whole world in front of her. It wasn't until she was around three years old that my ex-wife and I noticed she was falling behind. She had difficulty making friends and keeping up with other kids her age. She had to repeat Kindergarten and would often come home upset and defeated, which was unlike her. We wondered if her development was the cause of her being held back a year or something else. I had always suspected some issues regarding her teacher, so, being a protective parent, I snuck a tape recorder in my daughter's backpack and sent her off to school. Her teacher was horrible and would scream at my daughter and the rest of her class. After several other complaints and parent conferences with the school principal, she was forced to retire.

Unfortunately, my daughter had more obstacles in front of her. She was diagnosed with an auto-immune disorder and irritable bowel syndrome. Loud noises made her irritable, and she seemed to have impaired vision. As she grew older, she fell further behind in school, struggled with reading and test-taking, and was constantly bullied. She struggled with conceptual thinking, and she seemed to rely more on memorization to pass her classes rather than comprehending the information. She would often get caught in negative thought patterns and was later diagnosed with ADD and ADHD.

When my daughter was in 7th grade, we discovered her eyes were not tracking correctly. I didn't think twice about taking a second job to be able to pay for her physical therapy. Like any parent, I did everything possible to give her the best medical care. It broke me to see her struggling. We kept up with therapy appointments three times a week for an entire year, which resulted in dramatic improvement in her reading skills.

She learned how to do things in the best way for her; her ability and determination amazed me.

Taking Care of My Mom - Everything Coming Back Full Circle

When I was growing up, car seats were non-existent. Things were just different then. That being said, we used to drive over to my uncle's house to get our hair cut. One afternoon, while we were on our way, the rear passenger tire of my mom's car sheared off, and we lurched very hard to the right. "Jesus!" my mom called out as the car threw itself off the road. I remember sitting up and looking around. A man was running up to my mom's window. He had been driving his truck right behind us. I remember him telling my mom he was so glad he was on schedule with his route that day because he tends to speed when he runs behind and easily could have hit us. Of course, I was young and didn't understand much of what was being said. I do remember my mom's voice frantically calling out, "Jesus!" before we came to a stop. I wouldn't realize until much later in life that, at that moment, we were being looked after.

I went to the doctor's office shortly after that car accident, and that's when the doctor told my mother and father that I had hip dysplasia. I was three and a half years old.

My mom always taught me to put the needs of others before my own. She always looked out for me and never put herself first. During the last 15 years that my parents were together, my dad tried to be more health-conscious and gave up sweets. So, my mom did, too, because those are the things you do for those you love. When my dad was on his deathbed, I made a promise to him that I would take care of her. She deserved it after everything she did for our family. So that's what I did. In the years that followed, as her Dementia worsened, I took my mom on her first roller coaster, to her first Christian rock concert, and on a tour of Washington D.C., and I saw her experience swimming in the ocean for the first time. We had a bowl of ice cream together every night before bed. It was her turn to experience life's grand things, just as she always did for me.

She wasn't just a wonderful mother; she was a fantastic grand-mother. She would talk to my daughter and my daughter's friends about relationships, dating, and what she learned. She wished them a partnership like the one she had with their grandfather. She was never cruel or violent and never seemed to have a bad day. She was always in good spirits, even until the end. Hospice care was the only thing that allowed me to get some rest while I was taking care of her. The last two and a half years of her life were hard on both of us. My own family didn't do much to care for her or offer help when we needed it most. She became less mobile, but she was by my side in her wheelchair everywhere I went. Everything I did, she and I did it together.

For the last 36 hours of her life, she was no longer verbal and would communicate by blinking. Once for "yes" and twice for "no." She passed peacefully at 3:45 in the morning, about an hour after sending me away to get some sleep.

When I talk to my clients about caring for their parents, I often talk about my mom, reminded of the love she selflessly gave to me and those around her. I tell my clients that nothing is owed to us, and we don't step up in these situations out of obligation or a contract of some kind. In most cases, we are lucky to have parents who never let us feel lonely or sidelined. The best we can do in return is to be there and let them continue experiencing life with you. Spend time by the ocean, take city tours, and eat ice cream.

So when I have a conversation with you about being, Perfectly Imperfect, I can can speak from experience, listen with a purpose, and provide a solution with empathy. Looking forward to our next chat. With blessings, my prayer for you and your family is a life of abundance.

***

Author Bio:

Bill Walters is a compassionate financial advisor dedicated to helping families achieve economic security and peace of mind. As the founder of *Perfectly Imperfect Families*, he combines professional expertise with deep personal experience to guide clients toward stable financial futures.

Raised by a disciplined Navy father and a determined mother who instilled in him resilience and preparation, Bill learned early the value of hard work and responsibility. His childhood was marked by challenges, including a diagnosis of hip dysplasia that left him temporarily paralyzed and bedridden for long periods. Yet, through these struggles, he discovered perseverance—a trait that would define his personal and professional journey.

Bill's commitment to overcoming adversity continued into adulthood. After losing a track scholarship in college due to injury, he redirected his focus toward business and sales, where he embraced failure as a catalyst for growth. Later, as a father, he fought tirelessly to support his daughter through learning disabilities, health struggles, and systemic obstacles—reinforcing his belief in resilience and advocacy.

A defining chapter in Bill's life was serving as the primary caregiver for his mother during her battle with Dementia. This deeply personal experience taught him the profound importance of family, love, and planning for life's uncertainties.

Today, Bill channels these lessons into his work, helping families navigate financial planning with empathy and wisdom. His approach is rooted in the understanding that true wealth lies not just in numbers but in the security to cherish life's most meaningful moments. Through *Perfectly Imperfect Families*, he empowers clients to build legacies of stability, strength, and love—just as his parents taught him.

When he's not advising clients, Bill enjoys sharing his insights on resilience, caregiving, and financial empowerment. He ensures that every family he works with feels seen, supported, and prepared for whatever lies ahead.

Chapter 4

Business Growth Through Gratitude

Donna Grande

For more than 25 years, I navigated the demanding corporate highway of national sales, operating in the corporate fast lane—thriving, or perhaps merely surviving, in the relentless, high-stakes world of corporate America. Picture this: endless quotas, spreadsheets, strategy sessions, cold calls, and those regular "let's circle back" emails.

My days were filled with back-to-back meetings and persistent pressure to meet the ever-escalating

> 66
> "Build Relationships First...
> Relationships Are What Will
> Build Your Business"
> -Donna Grande
> 99

sales goals. It was all very --- transactional, mechanical, even robotic. Sure, I excelled professionally, and my office shelves boasted multiple awards and plaques, but behind these tangible marks of achievement lay an intangible sense of emptiness. Despite my outward success, I was acutely aware something essential was missing. I craved genuine connection. I didn't want to just *sell*, I wanted to **connect!**

Back then, the prevailing corporate mantra was simple and repetitive - we were taught that volume was everything – we were encouraged to make more cold calls, send more emails, and initiate more sales pitches. And while that method did bring in numerical results, it left me exhausted and unfulfilled. Selling had become a chore, and was lacking, real human connection. Deep within, I sensed that the core essence of meaningful interactions was missing. The constant emphasis on volume—more calls, more pitches, more meetings—felt hollow, increasingly unfulfilling. I vividly recall a particular evening when I was staring blankly at my computer. The thought came sharply into my mind, "There's got to be a better way".

And indeed, there was.

Little did I know, the better way was about to reveal itself - It didn't come in the form of another CRM or sales tactic. It came as a simple, heartfelt shift in perspective – and a tool that would transform how I did business. A tool that my friend, Steve Eanes shared with me as he welcomed me to my first Toastmasters meeting. Steve was utilizing this tool in his business and was so enthusiastic about sharing this unique tool with me. The minute Steve showed me this tool, I knew instantly it was my answer to unlocking genuine connections in business.

Boom! The tool that was shared with me was SendOutCards, a brilliant, heartfelt tool created by visionary entrepreneur Kody Bateman. This wasn't just a new tool; it was a new way of approaching business, rooted deeply in heartfelt appreciation. At its core, SendOutCards wasn't merely a service—it represented a revolutionary approach to business, one built entirely around authentic appreciation.

Kody's foundational principle was elegantly simple yet powerful: Listen deeply to your inner promptings, express sincere appreciation freely, embody gratitude consistently, and openly share that gratitude with others. This wasn't just another sales tactic—it was a new way of life. This resonated with me deeply, and it aligned perfectly with the unspoken longing I had carried for years.

Starting slowly, I integrated this gratitude-driven practice into my professional routine. Every LinkedIn connection, who were previously nothing more than accepting my invitation, was now met with a personalized, heartfelt thank-you card. This marked the beginning of what would soon become an entirely new business practice for me. Introductory meetings were no longer concluded with bland emails; instead, heartfelt cards conveying my sincere appreciation were created and sent. Birthdays? Check. Work anniversaries? Absolutely. Career changes? Congratulations were sent! Work promotions? I was cheering them on with personalized messages in cards that were mailed. Soon, I found myself sending out "just thinking of you" cards, too. I was on a roll—and it felt amazing.

But here's the real magic; my target audience started calling *Me*. My prospects, who were receiving my cards on a consistent basis and at once, were hesitant or sidestepping my calls and emails about who I was or what product or service I represented, now reached out proactively. Instead of ignoring my calls or emails, they eagerly engaged, expressing gratitude in return. Prospective clients saw me not as just another sales executive vying for their attention but as someone who truly valued them as individuals. They felt recognized, seen, and valued—and remembered. This was a far cry from the transactional and traditional cold calls and emails that they experienced daily. I wasn't just another name in their inbox; I was the one who sent them cards that made them smile because my messages in my cards were never selling, just building a relationship and showing kindness and appreciation. This is a lost art in this world and the world of selling. My simple acts of genuine care and gratitude had opened more doors for me than a thousand cold calls ever could.

This new way of connecting sparked a remarkable change. This shift underscored a fundamental truth I'd come to embrace-authentic connection through gratitude transcends traditional business methods every time. My relationships deepened, opportunities multiplied, and referrals soared.

Now, I was all about saving time, money and being proficient. This tool addressed all three concerns. When integrating this powerful tool into my daily practice, it amplified my ability to promptly and genuinely express gratitude in both my personal and professional interactions. It was a plug-n-play tool that made it so easy and user-friendly. Whether I was at an in-person meeting or connecting online, I could instantly act on my promptings. Using my phone during face-to-face meetings, I effortlessly sent personalized cards directly through an intuitive app. For virtual meetings, my laptop enabled me to easily select and customize cards from an extensive online catalogue.

Remarkably, within just a few minutes, I was able to choose an appropriate card, compose a heartfelt message, and press "submit." The rest was seamlessly handled—the cards were professionally printed, stamped, and mailed from their Salt Lake City office. This tool didn't just simplify my expressions of gratitude—it made them convenient and cost-effective as well. With such an easy-to-use and impactful solution at my fingertips, there was truly no reason not to send thoughtful, personalized cards consistently.

This new approach fundamentally shifted my entire business paradigm. It underscored a powerful truth: genuine connection through gratitude is profoundly more effective than traditional transactional methods. This shift ignited a newfound passion for me to create a sales strategy. A sales strategy with a complete set of best practices and a process that blended my corporate experience with this new, heart-centered approach in tandem with the 7-figure Follow-up Method by author, Jay Malloy. As I started working with Jay, as my life coach. His motto, "It all works. Just focus on consistently delivering a clear and honest message" reinforced my commitment to making meaningful connections through the power of follow-up. Most professionals lose valuable opportunities not because they lack skill or talent, but because they fail to follow up.

In this fast-paced world where people are constantly bombarded with messages, a thoughtful follow-up (message) can be the difference between being forgotten and being remembered. It shows professionalism, persistence, and genuine interest- qualities that build trust and deepen relationships. Without it, even the best first impressions fade quickly, and potential clients, partners, or referrals slip through the cracks.

I created what I now call, **The Grande Connector Method**—a system rooted in authenticity, consistency, and of course, gratitude. Additionally, an automated follow-up system that Jay Malloy set up, completes the "Grande Connector Method". It's a process that doesn't just grow business – it transforms it. It represents a transformative approach to business that emphasizes relationships first, knowing fully that such relationships naturally build thriving enterprises. An important goal that I share with business owners is that their goal should never be about fitting in, but their primary aim must always be ways to discover how to genuinely stand out.

In today's saturated market, businesses frequently attempt to blend in, thinking that conformity ensures acceptance and stability. But true success and impactful growth lie in daring to be different, memorable, and sincerely caring.

An idea I had and began initiating as part of The Grande Connector Method, is adding video to the personalized cards. Imagine being memorable and standing out by creating a 30-second video that shares your authentic message, a heartfelt thank-you or a quick introduction- and turning that video into a QR code. Place that code inside a personalized card you're mailing to your prospect or client. This simple touch engages four of the five senses: 1. they have to open the teal-colored envelope (so you will get a 100% open rate), 2. they feel the card, 3. read your words and then see and 4.hear you through your recorded video.

It's a powerful, multi-sensory way to stand out, build connection and be truly memorable in a world that's craving more personal, human touches. It resulted in building strong relationships, achieving appointments that I would have never secured without this process. I was elated with how I enjoyed the position of a Vice President of Sales at a National Facility Maintenance Company utilizing this tool and process.

Then came a pivotal moment. My beloved mother, Grace Grande, whose unwavering support and profound love shaped every aspect of my character, entered a nursing home. Not long after, she transitioned into hospice care. Life stood still for me. And in that quiet, sacred space and days that I spent by her side, my life came into sharp focus, illuminating a deeper calling I had felt being ignored for far too long. Amidst the quiet, profound days spent at her bedside, I finally embraced a deeper calling—one that had gently but persistently whispered to me for years.

You see, my Mom understood me deeply. She had always known how much I loved giving and my passion helping others, showing appreciation and connecting them to opportunities. She saw the joy I experienced when I sent thoughtful cards for "just because" to several folks. But more profoundly, she wasn't alone in recognizing this truth. God had been nudging me for a long time, whispering in my heart, that I was meant for something more – something that honored both the One whom I serve and the woman who had shaped me. I was destined for something greater, something aligned with my core, honoring the values my mother instilled in me.

So, just weeks before she passed, I did it! I started my company. I named it **Gratitude by Grace,** doing business as **GrandeConnections**- a tribute to the one I serve and the woman who inspired it all. I still remember the smile that spread across her face when I told her. We both cried – happy tears, sacred tears. It was a shared dream finally realized. The memory of sharing this decision with her, the radiant smile illuminating her face as joyful tears filled both our eyes, remains one of my most cherished moments.

And it was only the beginning. That moment marked not only the birth of my business but the beginning of an extraordinary mission: to help change the world one card at a time through coaching business professionals on how to achieve sustained growth by prioritizing genuine relationships over transactional interactions. Because, you see - I've lived both sides and I can tell you without hesitation—relationships win every time.

My unique approach, grounded firmly in gratitude, consistently generates exceptional results. Businesses adopting The Grande Connector Method regularly experience dramatic increases—in referral rates. Employee and customer retention improve significantly because people are drawn naturally toward genuine care and heartfelt appreciation. Gratitude becomes not just a business strategy but a joyful, uplifting part of the corporate culture.

Reflecting on my journey, gratitude permeates every aspect of my life. My heart is continually thankful: to God for providing clarity and guidance; to my mother, Grace, whose love profoundly shaped my character and purpose; to my husband, Scott Goroski, whose unwavering support fuels my entrepreneurial spirit; and to each connection that has enriched my journey.

And now, I want to share this process with others through my upcoming coaching program that is designed to walk you through the exact steps. My aim is clear: empowering you to transform connections into clients and clients into raving fans.

If you're tired of the endless grind of unanswered cold calls, numerous emails that end up in spam, unread or just get deleted with this impersonal outreach – you may be ready for a method that genuinely feels good, resonates authentically, and generates tangible, lasting results – then this is your invitation. Let's discuss how embracing gratitude-driven practices can revolutionize your business experience and it feels good too.

Remember to Build Relationships First ..... Relationships will Build your Business.

***

Author Bio:

Donna Grande brings over 25 years of dynamic experience as a VP of Sales for a major facility maintenance company, a seasoned franchise sales executive, and a strategic relationship specialist in mergers and acquisitions.

Through navigating high-stakes sales environments and complex corporate negotiations, Donna discovered the ultimate secret to sustainable success, captured vividly in her chapter, *"The Business of Growth through Gratitude,"* within the book *Cracking the Success Code - The Best Business Lesson I Have Ever Learned.*

Her journey highlights the transformative power of genuine relationships and gratitude, demonstrating that the most profound sales growth emerges not from transactions but from authentic human connections.

Call to Action: Take the first step today. Book your free 30-minute consultation with me at www.GrandeConnections.com and let's begin transforming your business with the gratitude-driven way.

Watch the ever-trending Gratitude Webinar: https://webinar.promptings.com/140761

Chapter 5

Escaping the Job from Hell

Jeff Pizzino

"Help! Help! I'm being repressed!"
— *Monty Python and the Holy Grail*

That line from *Monty Python and the Holy Grail* — shouted by the peasant Dennis as he's confronted by King Arthur — echoed in my head nearly every day during what I now refer to as "the job from hell."

It perfectly captured how I felt: frustrated, stifled, and stuck in an employment situation that was highly challenging, soul-sucking, and emotionally draining.

> "Whoever tells the best story wins."
> - Annette Simmons

But there was a silver lining. That miserable job experience in the early 2000s led me to discover the power of a killer elevator speech — and that single discovery turned everything around. A well-crafted elevator speech can open doors, whether you're looking for new employment or trying to close a new business deal.

More on that in a moment. First, let me set the stage for one of the most important lessons of my career...

PR Business Crashes and Burns

It was late summer 2001. We were living in the Salt Lake City metro area. After running my own public relations and marketing communications business for nearly 11 years, I was growing weary of entrepreneurship and considering a return to the nine-to-five world.

One of the biggest factors pushing me toward that decision was a local client who had recently stiffed me for a substantial amount of money. He owned a monthly commercial real estate publication I had rebranded as "*Utah Progress.*" I wrote all the stories and typeset the entire full-color publication. It had become the go-to source for Utah real estate news. It looked great — but it was a ton of work.

Then one month, he promised to pay me the following month with advertising revenue.

I made the mistake of being too trusting and believing.

He pressured me to continue producing the publication, promising to pay me the next month. It reminded me of the character J. Wellington Wimpy from the *Popeye* cartoons: "I'll gladly pay you Tuesday for a hamburger today." My client's version: "I'll gladly pay you next month for another issue of *Utah Progress* today."

Just like Wimpy, the promises kept coming.

As he repeated this line for four or five months, the unpaid amount kept adding up. My hope of getting paid was dashed when he finally told me he was shutting down the business and had no money. I was out several thousand of dollars.

This was actually the third time in five years I'd had a client refuse to pay what was owed — and this third time was anything but the charm. It killed my enthusiasm for entrepreneurship. And an unenthusiastic entrepreneur, especially one supporting a wife and four children, is a recipe for disaster.

Time to Put the Corporate Handcuffs Back On

I realized it was time to shelve my dream of being my own boss and return to the corporate world.

To make the transition more palatable, I decided I wanted to enjoy the beach and warmer weather of Southern California — where my wife had been born and raised. I knew she wouldn't mind the move.

Using my skills in writing persuasive sales copy, I crafted a killer, attention-grabbing cover letter to accompany my résumé and submitted it to various job postings on Monster.com.

In September 2001, I landed a job in the PR department at a large nonprofit educational institution. The campus in Carlsbad, California — about 30 miles north of San Diego — was stunning. The main lobby had breathtaking polished cement floors that looked like marble. My office even overlooked the Pacific Ocean.

This Wisconsin native thought he'd died and gone to heaven.

All Not So Well in SoCal

But I soon discovered I had landed in the *other* "H" word.

My new boss, the PR manager, was a former military officer. He wore a suit jacket — always buttoned — and a tie every day. And he always looked stressed.

While I appreciated his military service, I didn't appreciate the way he brought a military mentality into our department. I had entered a command-and-control nightmare.

Our three-person PR department included a young woman who, like me, found the environment difficult. Employees in other departments were wonderful — some became lifelong friends. I had just drawn the short straw.

My boss had no idea how to win the hearts and minds of his team. I seldom felt empowered or trusted — only micromanaged. He completely missed the mark on servant leadership, the kind rooted in trust, care, and empowerment.

The poor guy didn't seem very happy either. He often wore a furrowed brow, with veins popping out of his forehead.

One example is when we had weekly meetings with the marketing department, during which we were expected to report on our projects. My coworker and I had to submit our reports in advance so our manager could pre-approve them. He'd bring a copy of my agenda to the meeting. If I ad-libbed — straying too far from the script — I'd either get the evil eye during the meeting or a private "chat" afterward.

Written Up

One day, I learned the hard way that he had no sense of humor.

During one meeting, he mentioned the possibility of hiring interns. Later, someone said local school kids were visiting the campus for a field trip. I joked, "Hey, maybe they can be your interns."

The timing and delivery got laughs — from everyone except my boss.

He thought people were laughing *at* him. He officially wrote me up for insubordination and reported me to human resources. I explained it was just a lighthearted comment — no harm intended.

Didn't matter. He was insulted, and he unleashed his full wrath. Thankfully, he didn't have access to a firing squad.

My friends in other departments knew my boss's reputation. They felt sorry for me. I often visited the marketing manager for refuge and support. When I'd show up at his door, he'd smile and say, "Your manager again?" and invite me in.

And I'm sure my wife was tired of hearing me come home and complain about my boss every night. The despair and frustration were overwhelming.

After more than two years in this toxic culture, I knew I couldn't take it any longer.

Enter the Elevator Speech

Desperate to find a new job, I started applying to job postings and even spent a few thousand dollars on an executive search firm in Irvine. They also provided job interview coaching.

Turns out, the firm was a scam when it came to securing interviews. They claimed they blasted my résumé to hundreds of employers — but not a single interview resulted.

However, they *did* teach me one incredibly valuable strategy: have a polished elevator speech that sells your personal "sizzle." Once written, review it with trusted mentors, and rehearse it until it flows naturally — with genuine passion.

They helped me refine my speech and even recorded me delivering it so they could provide feedback.

Learning how to write and deliver an elevator speech was the *single* best takeaway from that firm. It made the entire experience — including their broken promises — worth it.

That skill turned out to be pure gold.

What Is an Elevator Speech?

An elevator speech summarizes what makes you tick. It highlights how your skills can help your target audience get what they want — and ideally answers, "Why should I hire you?"

Done well, it should leave the listener — a hiring decision-maker — slightly awestruck.

Going to an interview or networking event without one is like standing in an elevator with no buttons to push.

A carefully honed elevator speech is especially important when answering the inevitable question, "Tell me about yourself." The right speech can give you a serious edge over other candidates.

Putting the Elevator Speech to the Test

Penta Water, a bottled water company located just a few miles from my job in Carlsbad, had an opening for a PR manager. I applied using the same bold, attention-grabbing cover letter strategy I'd used before. I tailored my application to show how my skills not only matched but exceeded their requirements.

Boom. The VP of marketing, Dave Donaldson, responded. Interview secured.

I rehearsed my elevator speech over and over — probably 100 times. I was beyond motivated.

When I walked into Dave's office in April 2003, I was ready. He struck me as someone who liked to slightly intimidate people — but he was also easy to talk to.

No sooner had I sat down when he asked the golden question: "So, tell me about yourself."

The Penta Water Elevator Speech

My elevator speech has evolved, but this is how my first one went:

Thank you for this interview. You'll be interested to know I have over 15 years of experience in public relations. My forte is ensuring your company's communications have clarity, impact, and authenticity. I believe one of the most important PR principles for maximizing a company's success is embracing people-centered management practices.

I've worked for a top-10 PR agency in New York City, a Fortune 100 company, a large nonprofit corporation, and several startups.

My track record exemplifies high ethics and integrity, a natural flair for creativity and innovation, and strong organizational and problem-solving skills.

My background includes direct response advertising experience and more than 12 years of running my own PR business, so I'm very results-oriented. My major strengths lie in communicating your company's message clearly, following through on details, and demonstrating a passion for ensuring Penta Water's internal and external customers are informed and satisfied.

I hold a bachelor's degree in communications, with an emphasis in public relations, and I'm semi-fluent in Spanish.

In summary, the three main strengths I bring are:

   1. Versatility in PR, marketing, and management.

   2. A passion for creativity and innovation.

   3. An unwavering commitment to ethics and integrity.

I'm ready to help tell Penta Water's story.

By the time I finished, Dave was wide-eyed and clearly impressed. "Wow," he said.

Then: "Come with me."

He marched me upstairs to the COO, Ike Gill. "Tell him what you just told me," Dave said.

I repeated my pitch. Ike listened closely. After a few more questions, they thanked me and sent me on my way.

The next day, I got the call: I had the job.

The Power of a Polished Pitch

The joy and relief of escaping the worst work environment I'd ever experienced were indescribable. I wanted to dance on my old boss's desk and get written up again — but I didn't. (At least, I don't think I did.)

Penta Water became the most enjoyable corporate job I ever had. They empowered me to build the foundation for all corporate communications. I felt trusted — and free.

Later, I found out they had already offered the position to someone else. But Dave saw my cover letter and felt compelled to meet me.

When he heard my elevator speech, he rescinded the other offer and hired me instead.

That is the power of a finely honed elevator speech.

7 Tips for Nailing Your Elevator Speech

1. **Write for the ear** – Read it aloud. Record and listen. Does it flow? Is it easy to understand?

2. **Grab attention immediately** – Start strong. No "So, umm..." Open with your top skill or most compelling quality.

3. **Customize it** – Tailor it slightly for each role or audience.

4. **Sound natural, not memorized** – Rehearse it so well it flows like your favorite song.

5. **Use video rehearsal** – Record yourself and review your tone, body language, and habits.

6. **Keep it the right length** – About 1–2 minutes is usually perfect.

7. **Convey confidence** – Sit forward. Make eye contact. Smile. Use natural pauses. Be enthusiastic — but relaxed.

Bonus Tip:

If you're not asked, "Tell me about yourself," take the initiative. Politely ask, "Would you mind if I first take a minute to tell you about myself?" No reasonable interviewer will say no — and if they do, maybe that's not the place for you.

If you want your career to always be "going up," then a polished elevator speech is your best ride.

***

Author Bio:

Jeffery E. Pizzino, APR is a spin-free public relations pro who's passionate about telling the WHY of your story with clarity, impact and authenticity. He embarked on his PR career in 1987 at Ketchum Public Relations in New York City but has spent the majority of his career as a solopreneur.

He's <u>AuthenticityPR</u>'s Chief Authentic Officer and also functions as the fractional CCO for technology startup <u>Converus</u>. Jeff has an MBA in Management from Western International University and a Bachelor of Arts degree in Communications — with an emphasis in PR — from Brigham Young University.

This Milwaukee, Wisconsin native also holds an Italian citizenship. Jeff and storyteller wife Leticia have four children and four grandchildren. His hobbies include studying Italian, playing guitar, gardening, playing disc golf, reading, spinning New Wave/eclectic music, serving in his church, watching BYU football, and playing board games. Are your communications attention-getting, engaging and persuasive? Check out what we can do for you here: https://authenticitypr.com/wp-content/uploads/2023/12/AuthenticityPR-1-pager.pdf

Chapter 6

Hospitality: The Key to Success in any Business

Dan Casanta

I grew up in Youngstown, Ohio the grandson of Italian immigrants who came to the United States through Ellis Island. My father was one of eight children while my mother was one of nine. Both of my grandfathers held three jobs while both grandmothers worked at home; raising children making sure they were properly clothed, fed and well-behaved.

Both sets of grandparents instilled the values and morals that they felt their brood needed in order to be suc-

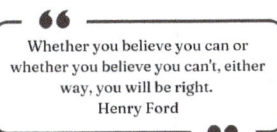

> Whether you believe you can or whether you believe you can't, either way, you will be right.
> Henry Ford

cessful and happy in life. If you followed those children; my parents and my uncles and aunts – they all found success throughout their lifetime. Yes, they had their ups and downs but because of their upbringing, they had plenty more successes than failures, more peaks than valleys and a strong faith to carry them through.

In my family, my two older sisters and I were taught and learned the same morals and values. Honesty, integrity, and standing up for what we thought was right. It was drilled into our heads that hard work pays enormous benefits. We were instructed <u>not</u> to follow the crowd and to be independent thinkers. Most importantly, they taught us right from wrong, and to always do the right thing. Lou Holtz, the legendary college football coach most notably at Notre Dame and South Carolina, stressed the importance of "doing the right thing". In a speech that he gave many years ago he stated that when you put your head on your pillow at night......you know if you did the right things that day. He also said "I follow three rules: Do the right thing, do the best you can, and always show people you care. You've got to make a sincere attempt to have the right goals to begin with, then go after them with appropriate effort, and remember that you can't really achieve anything great without the help of others."

My parents taught us manners and to respect our elders As a boy, I was taught to have a firm handshake and look people in the eyes. Smile. Be polite. Be nice. We were told to help others even if it was inconvenient. Do nice deeds and don't be afraid to go out of your way to someone's aid........even strangers.

These values did not stay within the confines of our family home; they extended into the way we approached everything in life, particularly in business. One of the fundamental lessons we absorbed was the paramount importance of treating customers and clients with unwavering respect. In a world where competition is fierce, and choices are abundant, hospitality becomes the defining factor that sets a business apart.

My father went into business for himself. Early on he opened a full-service gas station which grew over time to three locations. Self-serve gas stations weren't an option back then. I can remember pumping gas when I was nine or ten years old. As an added service, we cleaned the windows (not just the windshield), checked the oil and checked the tires for proper air pressure. Many stations just pumped the gas. My father said doing those basic things separated us from our competition and kept our customers coming back. And let's not forget the big smile and the big thank you to our customer before they pulled away.

Hospitality in business is not just about offering a polite smile or a courteous greeting; it is about creating an experience that leaves a lasting impression. When customers feel valued and respected, they are more likely to return and to recommend the business to others. This kind of loyalty and positive word-of-mouth is invaluable. It's a premium that cannot be bought but must be earned through genuine care and attention to each client's needs.

Respecting customers means listening to their feedback, understanding their needs, and going the extra mile to ensure their satisfaction. It means creating an environment where they feel comfortable and appreciated, whether they are walking into a store, dining at a restaurant, or engaging in a professional service. This level of hospitality fosters trust and builds a strong foundation for lasting relationships.

Recently, my family and I made the big move to North Carolina! Between unpacking what felt like a million boxes (kudos to my wife for handling most of it) and getting all the chaos of relocating squared away. Juggling the transition for both my business and my wife's—left me seriously overdue for a haircut! I found a barber with great reviews and only 10 minutes from home. Austin has been cutting hair since he was 18 years old and recently opened his own shop at age 31. He is a polite man, sincere as one could be and with me being a new customer he wanted to make sure he cut my hair to my satisfaction. What he said to me was another instance of hospitality and business. He asked about my family, work, and other personal details. It was great conversation and through my probing I learned more about him too. He talked about getting to know his customers, understanding not only how they want their haircut, but in essence who they are. He wanted to show his customers that they are important to him, hoping along with his skills as a barber that they will come back again and again.

Hospitality and respect are the keystones of a successful business. They are the values that transform a one-time transaction into a meaningful connection, encouraging customers to return time and time again. When a business prioritizes hospitality, it not only prospers but also creates a positive ripple effect that enriches the community it serves.

Author Will Guidara writes in his New York Times best selling book "Unreasonable Hospitality" that chefs at the finest restaurants in the world had long been celebrated for being unreasonable about the food that they served. Eleven Madison Park is a fine dining restaurant in the heart of New York City. Overlooking Madison Square Park–one of Manhattan's most beautiful green spaces–it sits at the base of a historic Art Deco building on the corner of East 24th Street and Madison Avenue.

Guidara tells the story of the General Manager at EMP who occasionally bussed tables which showed the team that he was there to help. As he was clearing a particular table, he overheard the guests crowing about the culinary adventures they'd had in New York: "We've been everywhere! Daniel, Pere Se, Momofuku, now Eleven Madison Park. The only thing we didn't eat was a street hot dog". The General Manager dropped the dirty dishes off in the kitchen and ran out to buy a hot dog from Abraham, who manned the hot dog cart on the corner.

He brought the hot dog back to the kitchen and asked Daniel the chef to plate it. The chef thought he was crazy, but he agreed to cut the hot dog into four perfect pieces, adding a swoosh of mustard, a swoosh of ketchup, and perfect quenelles of sauerkraut and relish to each plate. He approached the guest table and announced , "we're thrilled you chose us for your last meal in New York, but we didn't want you to go home with any culinary regrets," The servers set the artistically plated hot dog sections down in front of them. They were flabbergasted! Before they left one guest at the table told the General Manager that it was the highlight not only of the meal, but of their trip to New York. They'd be telling that story for the rest of their lives.

The story about Eleven Madison Park just proves that a little creativity and thoughtfulness can go a long way. It wasn't about some big, fancy gesture—it was just about listening to what the guests said and doing something cool for them. Who would've thought that a hot dog, of all things, could end up being the highlight of their trip? But that's the magic of paying attention and going the extra mile.

Acts of service like this work in any business. It's not about following a rulebook—it's about making people feel seen and special. When you do that, they remember it, they tell their friends, and they keep coming back. It's not rocket science, just good old-fashioned human connection.

Growing up, my dad's godfather, Vito, taught me that whatever you do, you should strive to be the best. Vito came to the U.S. from Italy with his mom at the turn of the century and started working in stone quarries when he was just 12. Later, he married Rosie, and they raised two boys who did well for themselves—one owned a construction company and the other became a pharmacist owning his own drugstore. Uncle Vito always told me, "I don't care if you make toothpicks—be the very best toothpick maker there is....or be nothing at all!" His sayings, like "shoot the rabbit when you see it" and "the harder you work, the better you feel," stuck with me. Between his wisdom and my father's high expectations, I quickly learned the value of hard work, finishing a job that you started, and doing it right. As I got older, I realized those lessons shaped how I would come to serve others.

My father sold his gas stations and pursued a career that coincided with his love for food, particularly Italian food. There was a chain of nine Italian delicatessens that were owned by one man in the Youngstown area. My father bought two of those stores and my two older sisters and I had the privilege (obligation) of working in the stores. At the tender age of eleven years old, I was in charge of the environment that is. I swept floors, took out the garbage and made sure all the products on the shelves and in refrigerated sections were arranged neatly and attractively. As I got older, I was a cashier and worked behind the deli counter waiting on customers while still being in charge of the environment. Just like we had in the gas station business we went over and above to serve our customers. I learned how a simple order of one pound of sliced salami had to be wrapped properly, neatly and handed to our customer with.... you guessed it, a big thank you and a smile. Along with doing everything as directed we had to be efficient and effective. On Saturdays, I worked from 8am to 6pm and I was exhausted!

Looking back, those lessons from Uncle Vito and my father weren't just about hard work—they were about hospitality, too. Whether it was wrapping up a pound of salami just right or making sure the store looked spotless, it was all about creating a welcoming experience for customers. My dad believed that every detail mattered, and that small touches, like a smile and a genuine thank you, went a long way in keeping people coming back. It wasn't just about selling food; it was about making customers feel valued.

That mindset of going above and beyond taught me the importance of thinking outside the box. Even simple gestures—like taking the extra time to make everything perfect—had a big impact on how people remembered us. Those early lessons showed me that hospitality isn't just a skill for restaurants or delis; it's a philosophy that can elevate any business by focusing on the people you serve and finding ways to exceed their expectations.

After college, I stepped into the real estate business, working for two brothers, Marty and Bill, who were close friends of our family. They were highly successful real estate brokers, builders, investors, and appraisers. When they asked me what I planned to do after graduation, I got the opportunity to join their team as a salesman. From day one, I saw how they built their success: through hard work, continuous learning, and most importantly, going above and beyond for their clients. This is where I first learned the true art of salesmanship—not by pushing for a hard sell, but by listening closely to clients, understanding their needs, and guiding them to a decision that felt right for them. It wasn't just about finding them a house; it was about helping them build a life they could afford in a place that suited their lifestyle.

Within two years, I had enough experience and successful transactions to take the broker's exam, which I passed at just twenty-three. However, the lessons I learned during those early days went beyond real estate. Marty and Bill taught me about relationships, community, and even faith. Though they were Jewish, and I am Catholic, they showed me the importance of giving back—not just to clients, but to the community and to God. Their example shaped not just my career but the values I carry with me every day. I owe a great deal of who I am to their mentorship.

When the economy in Youngstown, Ohio and across the Rust Belt took a downturn, it was time for a change. Thanks to my background in golf, I found a job as a sales rep in the golf industry. By the time I turned 31, I joined Titleist Golf as a regional manager and eventually worked my way up to overseeing custom markets. Titleist, known for being the number one golf ball on the PGA Tour and a leader in the marketplace, had a remarkable reputation, holding over 50% market share at the time. Despite the high demand for their products—like golf balls, clubs, and accessories—the culture at Titleist was deeply rooted in hard work, innovation, and, above all, taking excellent care of our customers.

Arrogance had no place in the company. Our mission was to be the best sales representatives and trusted partners of golf professionals and retail accounts. Every interaction was an opportunity to exceed expectations and reinforce the values that set Titleist apart. That culture of excellence and customer dedication is why Titleist remains at the top of the industry, paired with its world-class products.

When I started my own business, Cardinal Business Financing, Inc., I thought my background in business and finance, combined with everything I had learned from my previous jobs, gave me a solid foundation for success. What I didn't fully realize at the time was the incredible responsibility that comes with advising small business owners—people whose livelihoods and futures depended on the solutions I provided. It quickly became clear just how many small business owners were struggling to get the support they needed from traditional banks. Many were trying to scale their businesses but were held back by poor financial decisions or a lack of resources.

I drew on all the lessons from my past experiences and made it my mission to do more than just offer financing. My goal was to provide my clients with the tools they needed for sustainable growth, increased revenues, and peace of mind. Beyond offering financial solutions, I often connect my clients with other trusted professionals—CPAs, fractional CFOs, marketing experts, and more—who can help them achieve success. For me, this is about more than running a business; it's about serving others and making a real even if small, difference. Every day, I strive to embody that commitment, putting on my servant's hat and getting to work.

My family has been the cornerstone of my life, shaping who I am and how I approach the world. Growing up, we were taught that while friendships are meaningful, nothing surpasses the importance of family. I've embraced this belief in my own life, raising five incredible children and cherishing seven wonderful grandchildren. Ours is a blended family, a term we seldom use—with three grown children from my previous marriage, now thriving with families of their own, and two amazing twenty-year-old twins I share with my loving wife, Jane. Jane, raised in a strong Irish Catholic household, shares my deep-rooted appreciation for family and faith. She affectionately calls my daughters her 'bonus children,' and in our home, there are no distinctions of 'step' or 'half.' While we're not singing kumbaya every day, we are a unified family, rich with shared lessons, laughter, and love."

When I look back at all the lessons I've learned—about working hard, doing what's right, and striving for excellence—it's clear that these values have shaped not just my career but also how I approach life. Whether it was the values and integrity that I learned from my parents, Uncle Vito's wisdom, the mentorship from Marty and Bill, or the culture of excellence at Titleist, each experience taught me that the little things matter. Taking care of people, paying attention to details, and putting in the effort to go the extra mile—it all adds up.

The world could use more hospitality these days. A little more effort, a little more care, and a commitment to doing the job right can make all the difference. These qualities don't just create success; they build trust, relationships, and lasting impressions. For me, it all comes down to this: when you focus on your values and take care of others, good things tend to follow. It's a simple idea, but one that's stuck with me every step of the way.

***

Author Bio:

Dan Casanta, President and Founder of Cardinal Business Financing, Inc., has dedicated his career to empowering small businesses through tailored financial solutions.

Drawing inspiration from his upbringing and family values rooted in hard work and hospitality, Dan views every client interaction as an opportunity to build lasting relationships based on trust and respect.

With a deep understanding of the unique challenges small business owners face—whether in healthcare, construction, or manufacturing—Dan approaches financing with empathy and ingenuity. He founded Cardinal Business Financing, Inc., to break away from rigid, outdated processes, pioneering a model that prioritizes accessibility, efficiency, and meaningful service. "At Cardinal, we see our clients as partners, not transactions. Our servant-leadership approach drives us to exceed expectations and make financing a seamless part of business growth."

Leveraging his own entrepreneurial experience, Dan creates solutions that enable businesses to thrive and scale. He travels across the country to personally connect with clients, embodying the value of hospitality at every step. When not advocating for small business success, Dan takes an active role in community service, reflecting his commitment to giving back and nurturing relationships.

Based in Pinehurst, North Carolina, Dan lives with his family and continues to lead with integrity, vision, and a servant's heart.

Chapter 7

A Journey to Excellence

John Kalusniak

E xcellence isn't a trophy you stick on a shelf. It's a brutal, relentless grind that'll kick your ass and test your guts.

Forget the shiny motivational posters—this is about clawing through the muck, facing the crisis

> **"**
> "Great moments are born from Great Opportunities!! That's what you have here, that's what you have earned here........"
> -- Herb Brooks
> **"**

head-on, and coming out the other side tougher than nails. You don't get there by luck or talent. You earn it by refusing to quit when every fiber of you screams to tap out.

Lincoln said it best: "It's not the years in your life that count. It's the life in your years." Time doesn't give a damn about you—excellence comes from how hard you swing; how much you bleed for it. Every punch you take, every time you eat dirt, it's forging you into something unstoppable—if you've got the guts to keep going.

I've been there. I grew up scrapping on Detroit's mean streets, then slugging it out in the cutthroat business world. I've built empires from nothing and watched them crash and burn—over and over. Regrets? Hell no. Every failure was a street fight that taught me how to hit back harder. They'll do the same for you, but only if you stop whining and start swinging.

This isn't for the "success" chasers who just want a pat on the back. It's for the stubborn folk who know real wins come from getting battered and still standing. I'm here to drag you through this with me. You're not alone, but don't kid yourself—this fight's all on you.

Let's go. Dig deep, grow a spine, and get it through your skull: excellence isn't handed out like candy. You carve it out of the chaos with every damn choice you make. Welcome to the real *Journey to Excellence*.

The Foundation: Build It or Break

Excellence isn't some happy accident. It's a fortress you hammer together with blood, sweat, and no shortcuts. This isn't a one-and-done deal—it's a war you wage every day. Without a rock-solid base, you're just building a house of cards waiting to get flattened.

Forget the fake Instagram hustle. Excellence isn't how you look—it's what you do when no one's watching, when it's just you and the grind staring each other down. Talent? That's a cute bonus. What matters is grit and showing up when you'd rather crawl into a hole. Most people flake out here—they want the glory but can't stomach the mud.

Pillar one: Discipline. It's doing the work when you're dead tired, when the couch is calling, when excuses sound really sweet. No whining, no "I'll do it tomorrow"—just shut up and get on with it.

Pillar two: Commitment. Everyone's hyped at the start, but when the hits keep coming and the wins dry up, the quitters bail. Commitment's what keeps you in the ring when you're bruised and bleeding.

Pillar three: Hard Work. Excellence doesn't come cheap. It's late nights, early mornings, and giving a damn when no one else does. Half-ass it, and you're out.

I learned this the hard way. Early on, I strutted into a leadership gig like I owned the place—thought I'd flip it overnight with zero prep. Big surprise: it tanked. Teams checked out, goals went to hell, and I ate a big slice of humble pie. You can't fake the foundation. Build it right or watch it all collapse.

Rocky Balboa didn't lie: "The harder the battle, the sweeter the victory." You want it? Earn it with discipline, commitment, and sweat. Anything less, and you're just playing dress-up.

What're you building—a flimsy front or a bunker that takes a beating and stands tall? Your call.

Embracing the Grind: No Glamour, Just Guts

Everyone loves the spotlight—clapping, cash, clout. But talk about the grind—the ugly, endless slog—and they scatter like roaches. Excellence isn't about the highlight reel; it's about slugging it out in the trenches when giving up makes perfect sense.

Most don't fail because they suck—they fail because they quit. They start loud, all big talk and hype, but when the grind hits, they're ghosts. The ones who win? They're the crazy bastards who keep swinging when the crowd's gone home.

The grind's a beast. It's 4 a.m. wake-ups, gut-wrenching calls no one else will make, focus when the world's a circus. No one's cheering. No one cares. It's you versus you.

I thought I had it made once—big deals, street cred, the works. Then it all froze. Phones stopped ringing, deals died, and every step felt like wading through quicksand. Soul-crushing? Damn right. Most would've walked. I doubled down. You don't quit mid-fight—you grit your teeth, adapt, and push. The grind weeds out the weak.

Gretzky nailed it: "You miss 100% of the shots you don't take." Keep shooting, even when you're bricking. Winners don't wait for a pep talk—they grind it out in the dark, where no one sees. When the wall hits, do you fold or smash through? Excellence picks the fighters.

Persistence and Adaptability: Bend or Break

Excellence isn't a straight shot—it's a jagged, messy brawl. You don't get to coast. You either adapt, or you're roadkill.

People ditch their dreams when life goes sideways, crying it's "not meant to be." Screw that. Success isn't dodging the fall—it's crawling out of the pit every damn time. Excellence is getting up, not staying up.

I got schooled on this early. Had a sales game that crushed it—until it didn't. Market shifted, buyers ghosted, and I was left swinging at air. I clung to the old playbook too long, bleeding chances. Finally, I woke up, dissected the mess, and rewired everything. It sucked, but it worked. Stubbornness without flex is a death sentence—real strength is evolving while you bleed.

Lombardi said it: "It's not whether you get knocked down, it's whether you get up." Getting up means eating the lesson, not the loss. Adjust, keep moving. The greats don't bitch about change—they own it. You ready to shift gears when the wheels fall off, or just make noise about it? No retreat—just fight smarter.

Mentors and Teamwork: You're Not Rambo

Think you'll hit the top solo? Wake up. Even the baddest asses lean on someone. Excellence isn't a lone-wolf fantasy—it's forged with mentors who've been in the shit and teams who've got your back.

The "self-made" myth is for suckers. Every champ had a coach, an advisor, someone calling out their blind spots. My mentors ripped me apart—tough love that made me better. Teams? You're only as good as the crew you roll with. Lone rangers burn out.

I tried the solo act once—controlled everything, carried it all. Crashed hard. Only when I stopped being a jackass and built a real squad did I break through. Helen Keller wasn't kidding: "Alone we can do so little; together we can do so much." You need grit, sure, but you also need people who'll shove you past your limits.

Look at your crew. Are they lifting you or dragging you down? Got mentors kicking your ass forward? If not, fix it fast. No one climbs Everest alone.

The Price: Pay Up or Shut Up

Excellence isn't free—it'll cost you everything. Don't buy the "easy win" fairy tale. Long hours, missed birthdays, strained ties—it's a butcher's bill. You ready to bleed for it?

Everyone wants the crown—the shine, the rush—but the second it's about real sacrifice, they're out. No cheat codes. "The only easy day was yesterday." Deal with it.

I've paid in full. Skipped sleep, ditched parties, watched friendships fray—all for the bigger fight. Hit rock bottom when a deal I banked on imploded—money gone, faith shaken. I could've stayed down. I didn't. Muhammed Ali got it: "I hated every minute of training, but he said, 'Don't quit. Suffer now and live the rest of your life as a champion.'" The grind's brutal, but the payoff's worth it.

You in or out? Pay the price, or don't waste your time. The reward matches the pain—but only if you've got the stomach for it.

Call to Action: Step Up or Step Off

Excellence doesn't stumble into your lap. It's a gut-check you earn by outworking, outlasting, and outfighting the rest. I've laid it bare—now it's on you. Most won't cut it—they'll bitch, slack, and settle for crumbs. You want more? Prove it.

No excuses. "Later" is for losers—circumstances don't care. Past wins? Old news. Go all in or get out.

Link up with the real ones—mentors who'll smack you straight, crews who'll push you. Drop the dead weight.

Outwork everyone. Talent's nothing without sweat. Grit and hustle win.

Eat failure alive. It's coming—use it, don't lose to it. Adapt and charge.

Become a damn fortress. Discipline that doesn't bend, skills that shut mouths, habits that don't break.

Lombardi was right: "If we chase perfection, we can catch excellence." You gonna pay up, or just talk a big game? The world's full of dreamers—few got the spine to back it up.

Your move. Do it.

***

Author Bio:

As a Fractional Chief Revenue Officer with SalesXceleration, John has empowered organizations to shatter revenue ceilings, build high-performing sales teams, and turn underperforming operations into industry leaders.

His hands-on approach combines strategic insight with a relentless focus on execution, delivering measurable results for companies across diverse sectors.

John's philosophy is rooted in his Detroit upbringing—a city known for its resilience and work ethic. He believes that success isn't a gift; it's earned through grit, discipline, and an unwavering commitment to improvement. His passion lies in unlocking the potential of individuals and teams, pushing them to surpass their limitations and achieve extraordinary outcomes. John's no-nonsense style cuts through excuses, focusing on actionable strategies that drive real change.

In his chapter, *Journey to Excellence*, John distills decades of hard-won lessons into a powerful guide for anyone ready to elevate their game. This isn't a collection of abstract theories—it's a roadmap forged in the trenches of sales, leadership, and personal growth. From navigating high-stakes challenges to building a mindset that thrives under pressure, John's insights are practical, direct, and battle-tested. For John, excellence isn't found in comfort zones—it's forged in adversity, fueled by determination, and sustained by the will to keep pushing forward.

John's mission is clear: to inspire and equip others to take ownership of their journey, break through barriers, and achieve greatness. With John's guidance, the path to excellence is yours to conquer.

Chapter 8
The Imitation Trap

Angel Hicks

The realization that I didn't really know myself didn't hit right away. It was more of a gradual lesson I would learn over a decade of transforming into a serial entrepreneur. A lesson I will never completely finish learning.

It all started in 2013 when I got thrust into professional networking. I didn't stumble into it or realize I needed it by hearing someone else's success or getting invited to try it by a caring friend. No… I was thrust into it. I was a single mom of three kids for the last five years working 50 hours a week at a dead end sales job. I loved that job but needed something new. I had been there for 10 years and I was bored with a capital "B".

> "Life begins outside your comfort zone"
> - Neal Diamond Walsch

After months of complaining (you know…not doing anything about it but complaining), my mother decided to introduce me to a man who owned a local networking group called "The Business Network" (it has since been rebranded as H7 Network). At first I was like, "No way, Mom…I know what you're doing and I'm going to die happy and alone. I don't want to jump in the dating pool because the pool is poisonous." Her response after a major eye roll? "Quit being ridiculous. Just meet the guy! He may know people who are hiring for sales. He's got a huge network and he may be able to find you a new job." Oh... ok, fine, that sounds legit. So a few weeks before Christmas in 2013, Clay Hicks and I met for a one-to-one. I had no idea what a one-to-one was so I required my mother to go with me (I swore this was not going to be a date!) and soon realized I didn't need her there. We hit it off.

Of course, lighting struck us both that night and three months later, we were engaged. Six months after that, we were married. To say the least, I did not see that coming. I had created a list of everything I wanted in a partner and I was not going to settle. Clay checked every box. At this time I was a wallflower shy introvert. I did much better one on one and not being the center of attention. I was happy sitting quietly in the corner but I knew God was calling me to grow outside my comfort zone. Even though my zone had wine and great books, I still needed to grow or I was going to die alone in that little box.

I decided to create an agency of executive assistants. We would work in three silos: Processes and Procedure, Bookkeeping, and Data Entry. I grew a thriving business with other assistants working with clients in person and virtually. About a year later, I sold my business and at my husband's request, took over the only women's group in TBN (now H7) and revamped it to Evolve Women's Network.

In those early years of entrepreneurship, the transition period was brutal. I went from being told what to do eight to ten hours of my day to not having anyone guide me at all. My day used to be scheduled, my tasks were known, and my outcome was predictable. I'm sure many of you reading this can relate. I had to completely train myself to learn how to manage the time I was given. They call it "time management" but you can't manage time. You can only manage yourself in the time you've been given. Not only was I a new wife and entrepreneur, but I was also a new mom to two beautiful bonus daughters. We had four girls and a young son blending families and lives all at the same time. Three of those girls were in high school. It was only by the grace of God we all survived! Learning what tasks needed to be done when, how to balance my business and the responsibilities of my home life was one of the hardest things I've had to learn to do.

But here I was, chasing success like never before. Handling life and chasing dreams. I was watching what everyone around me was doing in business. How they were talking on the phone, how they were scheduling their time, how they sounded in networking meetings. And I wanted to be successful like they were. I wanted to be polished and professional. I was polished and professional in my old role but this was new. These people weren't working to build someone else's dream, they were working to build their own. I desperately wanted to be seen as one of them. So I changed the way I talked. I changed the way I interacted. I changed the way I introduced myself. I changed the time that I woke up. I was slowly killing myself and I didn't know it.

After years of trying to be someone else, I realized I was crashing and burning. I was burning out. I was reactive not responsive, I dropped into depression more often than normal, I put self care on the back burner and no longer did things that brought me joy. I knew then that something had to change. I knew I didn't want to change *who* I was, but *how* I was. The best business lesson I ever learned was to never stop learning about myself. How I work and who I am.

For the next several years, I looked into myself. I was growing Evolve and expanding into new states. I was working in H7 with my husband, serving on leadership teams, selling memberships, and growing there as well. I was building relationships and growing groups, I was polished and professional. I started taking every personality test I could get my hands on. Not because I wanted to put myself in a box of "That's just how I operate" but to figure out how I operate. With every test I took, I felt more liberated than the day before. I was looking into my natural habits and how I could adjust my behavior to make my weaknesses less of challenges and more of strengths.

I share all of this to encourage you to do the same—to take a long, honest look within. Not to label yourself or justify where you are, but to truly understand how *you* operate. What makes you come alive? What patterns serve you, and which ones hold you back? Self-awareness isn't about limitations—it's about liberation. The more you know about yourself, the more empowered you become to make choices that align with who you are at your core. Whether in business, relationships, or personal growth, the greatest transformation begins when you stop trying to fit into someone else's mold and start becoming the most authentic version of yourself.

The Conversation That Changed Everything

At this time I was pivoting and grinding. I was killing it at being a wife, a mom, an entrepreneur but I still couldn't quite put my finger on what was missing. I was still struggling to find my footing and wanted to expand my knowledge so I decided to become DiSC certified. DiSC is an assessment tool that helps individuals understand their strengths and weaknesses. "D" stands for Dominance, "I" stands for Influence, "S" stands for Steadfastness, and "C" stands for Conscientiousness. I realized that I was an introverted "S". I'm steady, I like the details, I'm dependable, and I like calm. Getting certified allowed me to connect with others better, sell better, and get a better understanding of what worked for me.

I really wanted to dig even deeper and reach higher so I took the next natural step... I hired a business coach. As our conversations progressed, the theme remained the same. "What do YOU want your life to look like? How do YOU process information and how do YOU want to grow your business?" That conversation smacked me like a ton of bricks. How *do* I work best? What *do* I want for my business and my life? I was so used to doing everything the way someone else was doing it. I was trying to grow in assertiveness, trying to be more dominating. Which in the grand scheme of things, wasn't a *bad* thing. It just wasn't the *right* thing.

Knowing who you are and how you operate is a gift only you can give.

What a concept! I don't have to be like someone else to make all this work? I know this sounds silly to someone who may have never lived like this. Never had self doubt, someone who has never struggled to feel like you fit in. But that was my experience. And now I gave myself permission to do it differently. I can't change anything I don't have control over but I have control over myself. So I started there. I was reinvigorated and energized. I was going to change my life.

Have you ever thought to yourself "This is the next thing! It's going to change the way I do business. Yep, this is it!" Yeah, I did that about a dozen times in the next year. I set up new programs and processes, I bought courses that did not in fact change the trajectory of my life. At first I was discouraged. I perceived that year as such a waste of time, money, and resources but it wasn't a waste. It was a crash course in what worked and what didn't. I learned so much about myself and how I work. I was becoming more productive. I was selling more and building deeper relationships. I started talking in meetings using language and words that were more natural to me and I was getting better responses. That one question... What do YOU want?... changed everything for me.

When was the last time you looked around your business, your office, or your house and asked yourself "What do *I* want it to look like? Is this serving *me*?" If it's been awhile, I encourage you to do that today. There's no time like the present. There's an old Irish proverb that says "There are many days in the grave for us." It's a reminder to live boldly, take chances, and embrace opportunities while we can, because life is short. It encourages us to be fearless and make the most of every moment.

Saying No With Confidence

In 2018 I was nominated by a networking connection for "Woman of the Year", an award put on by our local Leukemia & Lymphoma Society. At first, I was ecstatic! Can you imagine what just being nominated would do for my influence and visibility?! This was so exciting! Then I took a breath and asked myself what does this actually require of me? I scheduled a meeting with the campaign chair. I wanted to see what I have to do to actually win this award. She explained to me that each nominee would put together a team of 5-7 individuals who would then go and fundraise for the campaign. The team that acquired the most donations would be the winner. It was a healthy competition for a good cause. Except I knew myself much better by this point. My entire platform was based on collaboration among women, not competition. I knew that competition, healthy or otherwise, is not my thing and trying to win a popularity contest was going to be disastrous for all involved. Had this offer come several years earlier, I would have happily agreed to do it and probably failed miserably. This year I knew better so I politely declined.

Are there things that you are doing right now that don't fit your personality or that are causing you stress? Something you agreed to do but doesn't feel right? Are you living fearlessly and making the most of every moment or are you going through the motions in something that no longer serves you? Now is the time to assess *where* you are and *who* you are to create the life you want to live.

The Shift in Identity:

I've been an entrepreneur for over 11 years now. I no longer chase perfection or strive to be anyone other than myself. I am a lifelong learner who is constantly evolving, changing, and shifting. I am currently in the process of reinventing myself...again. Getting closer by the day to the authentic woman God created me to be. I've become obsessed with living in peace and joy my way.

Over the years, I've launched businesses that achieved success by many standards—profitability, growth, recognition. But what I've come to understand is that success alone isn't always the destination. Time and again, I've found myself looking back on those accomplishments and realizing I was ready for something new. Not because they failed, but because they no longer felt like a true reflection of who I am. Somewhere along the way, the spark faded. The passion shifted. The business may have still been thriving, but I wasn't.

Some of that restlessness, I now know, is tied to my ADHD—and knowing that has been a powerful revelation. It has helped me understand that my desire to evolve, to explore new challenges, isn't a flaw. It's a feature. It's how I'm wired. And more importantly, it's how I grow.

Sure, my path may look winding, unconventional, maybe even slower than others. But I've learned that no one's journey is a straight line—and that's okay. There's no universal roadmap to fulfillment. The only map that matters is the one you create for yourself.

So I encourage you to pause and reflect. Look inward. Examine your business, your side projects, your volunteer roles, even your family obligations. Ask yourself: What truly lights your soul on fire? Where do you feel most alive? Most aligned? Are you showing up each day as your most authentic self—or simply going through the motions of what once felt right?

This might just be the most powerful business lesson I've ever learned: success means nothing if it isn't yours.

***

Author Bio:

Angel Hicks is the founder of both Evolve Women's Collective and Infinite Impressions Publishing, where she wears the hats of Certified Publisher and Certified Author's Guide.

Through Evolve, she has cultivated a dynamic, judgment-free network for professional and entrepreneurial women—a space where growth, real conversations, and collaboration are always in style. At Infinite Impressions Publishing, Angel helps authors and thought leaders bring their book concepts to market in a third of the time and at a third of the cost. Her dedication and impact have earned her recognition as a Marquee's Who's Who Honored Listee (2024), Best Women's Group in Cincinnati (2021) by *Cinci Chic*, an Amazon Best Selling Author, and VP of Membership for the Downtown Morning Toasters, a club of Toastmasters International.

When Angel founded Evolve nine years ago, her vision was clear: to create a space where women could connect by sharing who they are—not just what they do. She noticed that so many of us are asking the same questions: how do I grow my business? How do I network more effectively? How do I attract the right clients? Instead of struggling alone or searching in silence, Angel believes in the power of community and shared wisdom. That spirit of connection naturally led to her passion for publishing—when the opportunity arose to edit and publish real stories, it was a perfect fit for her lifelong love of the written word.

Being part of this anthology is a meaningful reminder that growth in business—and in life—is never a straight line. Angel believes that stumbling blocks and mistakes are often the best teachers, and that success comes from doing the hard things, even when we don't feel ready. Her chapter, along with the stories shared by fellow contributors, reflects the truth that no one takes the escalator to the top—we all climb, one step at a time. Angel hopes readers walk away feeling encouraged, seen, and reminded that they're never alone on the journey.

You can connect with Angel via email at **Angel@EvolveWomensNetwork.com** or **InfiniteImpressionsPublishing@gmail.com**, and follow her professional journey on LinkedIn at www.linkedin.com/in/angelhicks.

Chapter 9

Sales Infastructure

Roy De Medeiros

B ob's office was unusually quiet that morning. The phones were still ringing, but slower than usual. The office energy—once charged—had dipped. Five consecutive quarters of flat or declining sales will do that to a team. Bob sat at the edge of his desk, flipping through a report he already knew by heart. Numbers were down. Again.

That's when Jim walked in.

A trusted advisor, Jim had the kind of presence that made it easy to talk

> 66
> "Give me a lever long enough and a fulcrum on which to place it, and I shall move the world.
> — Archimedes
> 99

about tough things. Bob had invited him in—not for motivation, but for a turnaround.

"Morning," Jim said, setting his notepad down. "You've built something good here; solid product and loyal customers. But something is missing."

Bob nodded. "It feels like we've hit a wall. The team's working hard, but we're not getting traction."

Jim pulled up a chair. "Let me ask you something, Bob. When you look at your pipeline right now, how confident are you in the deals closing this quarter?"

Bob paused. "Honestly? Not very. We've had deals stall out at the last minute. A couple vanished without warning."

"Do your reps log why those deals are stalling? Any visibility on bottlenecks?"

Bob shook his head. "Not really. It's mostly anecdotal. I hear bits and pieces, but no real data."

Jim nodded. "You're trying to build a home without a solid foundation. We need to step back and put the right structure in place—the kind that can support long-term growth."

"So where do we start?"

Jim opened his notepad. "With the missing a proper sales foundation. Most companies try to grow without proper sales infrastructure. It's the behind-the-scenes stuff that separates growth from grind."

He continued, "We reviewed *4,425 small to mid-sized businesses. Only 1% had an excellent sales foundation.*"

Bob blinked. "That's... not great."

"No, it's not. But *98% of companies that put a real sales foundation in place see an increase in visibility, reviews, and sales. On average, a 32% jump.*"

Jim flipped the page. "Let me show you something else. According to the Bureau of Labor Statistics, 20.8% of small businesses fail in the first year. Half don't make it past year five."

"And you're saying sales is the reason?"

"In many cases, yes. Of the *top ten reasons businesses fail*, five tie directly to sales: *no accountability, no visibility, lack of leadership, low sales.*"

Bob crossed his arms. "Sounds like us...so what's the fix?"

"Four pillars: Sales Strategy, Sales Process, Sales Analytics, and Sales Team Structure."

Jim flipped again. "Let's start with **Sales Strategy**. This is your blueprint."

"How are you currently deciding which markets or segments to pursue?"

Bob shrugged. "It's mostly gut feel. We try things based on referrals or industry chatter."

"And what about your top clients? Are you getting repeat business or just one-offs?"

"A mix. But we don't track that formally. We know who's big, but we've never done a full account review."

Jim nodded again. "Most companies try to scale without a strategy. They chase growth without knowing where it's coming from or who they're targeting."

Bob nodded. "We've never documented any of that."

"You're not alone. *Eighty-six percent of businesses struggle* with it. A real strategy starts with understanding your positioning. Are you the low-cost option, the premium one, or the disruptor?"

Bob paused. "Honestly? I don't think we've defined it."

"Then we'll define it together.

Next phase, we assess your total addressable market—your TAM. That gives us the real size of the opportunity. Without it, you're either playing too small or overreaching."

"Yeah. We've gone after leads that didn't make sense."

"And we fix that. Then we look at competitors—not to obsess, but to differentiate. If they're weak on service, that could be your edge."

He flipped the page. "Your CRM? It's more than a contact list. It should track activity, manage leads, generate quotes, and preserve data. We'll also examine your pricing—are you value-based or just reacting to the market?"

Bob looked thoughtful. "More reaction than strategy."

"We'll align it.

Next step we define your *unique selling proposition*. What makes you different? Your team should answer that in one sentence."

Bob leaned forward. "What about key accounts? We have big clients but no plan."

"That's part of the strategy. We identify top accounts, categorize them, and invest in the ones that drive long-term value. And we craft a value proposition—what you do, who you do it for, how you're different."

"And stay focused on the right audience," Bob added. "We've chased the wrong ones."

"Exactly. Strategy keeps you focused."

Jim leaned back. "This is where we start. After that, we move into Sales Process. That's where strategy turns into action."

Bob sat quietly, nodding. "Let's do it. I'm tired of guessing."

Jim smiled. "Good. Let's build your foundation."

The next morning, Bob met Jim with fresh coffee and a full notepad.

"I want to see what that blueprint looks like in action."

Jim nodded. "That's what the second pillar is about—**Sales Process**. It's where your blueprint becomes your build."

He pulled out a clean sheet. "From the same study we reviewed the other day, *74% of the companies who completed the survey did not have a documented sales process*. That's like giving someone a map with no destination."

Bob chuckled, but not with amusement. "We're totally in that group. Every sales representative does what worked before. No system."

"That's the issue," Jim said. "Without a process, you can't repeat success or fix failure. It's just guesswork. A well-defined process is the assembly line of your revenue engine."

He sketched on the pad. "These stages: Prospecting, Discovery, Qualification, Proposal, Negotiation, Close. At each one, we define what's required to move forward."

"And this works for any business?"

"We tailor it. A five-person shop and a hundred-person firm need different details—but both need structure."

Bob nodded. "How do we make sure the team follows it?"

"That's where your *CRM* comes in."

Bob raised an eyebrow. "We have one. We just... don't really use it."

Jim didn't flinch. "You're not alone. CRM isn't just software—it's your command center. It tracks deals, forecasts revenue, shows bottlenecks, and protects your data."

"That's also critical for forecasting and coaching," he added. "With real data, you know if you're in trouble long before the quarter ends."

Bob leaned back. "We've never used quotas well. We just make up numbers."

"Which is why you need *KPIs*. Leading and lagging indicators: calls made, meetings booked, pipeline growth, close rate. These aren't just numbers—they're signals."

"It would be great to have that kind of visibility," Bob said. "Right now, we find out we missed the quarter... at the end of the quarter."

"We'll fix that. We also need to clarify territories. If reps don't know what they own, they overlap or under-serve. We draw lines—geography, industry, or customer segment. And rules of engagement to reduce friction."

Bob scribbled notes. "That probably helps with morale too."

"Big time. When reps trust the system, they stop competing with each other and start competing with the market."

Jim stood. "Let me leave you with this—*structure doesn't kill creativity*. It enables it. When your reps know the path, they can focus on people, not process."

Bob nodded. "We've been running on hustle. Time to build a machine."

Jim smiled. "Exactly. And once we've got that, we'll move into the third pillar—**Sales Analytics.**"

Bob pushed the notes across the table. "Let's do it."

A week had passed, and Bob could already feel the shift. His team had started documenting their steps, using the CRM more deliberately, and asking better questions. But Jim wasn't ready to slow down.

They met again in the same conference room, this time surrounded by laptops and dashboards.

"So," Jim began, pulling up a spreadsheet, "let's talk about what's really going on inside your sales engine. That brings us to the third pillar—**Sales Analytics**."

Bob exhaled. "This is the one I've been nervous about. We've got numbers, but we're not using them. Not really."

"Exactly," Jim replied. "*From the same 4,400 companies surveyed, 94% had individual sales goals that didn't add up to the company's targets. Half had no dashboard. Two-thirds weren't tracking performance in a useful way.*"

Bob raised his eyebrows. "That many?"

"Even worse," Jim added. "*Seventy-six percent of managers and reps couldn't agree on what 'good activity' looked like. And most comp plans? They didn't reinforce the right behavior.*"

Bob shook his head. "We've been guessing. I thought it was just us."

"It's not. But it's fixable. Sales analytics helps us move from hunches to clarity. We'll start with a dashboard: pipeline health, deal velocity, win rate, and conversion points."

"We've talked about dashboards before," Bob said. "But it always felt too complicated."

"It doesn't have to be. Tools like HubSpot, Salesforce and Tableau have templates. We start small. Scale over time. Track activity and outcomes. If we only look at closed revenue, we're always too late."

"This would make coaching a lot easier," Bob said.

"It does. And it helps with *compensation plans*. Right now, you probably just pay on closed revenue."

"Correct."

"You should also reward reps for expanding existing accounts and landing new ones. Different skills, different incentives."

Bob nodded, scribbling notes. "We've never split it that way. Makes sense."

"Then we *segment accounts*. A-level: high value, high potential. B-level: solid growth. C-level: maintain or transition." This helps the sales representative manage their time and energy on the right accounts.

Jim stood and moved to the whiteboard. "Next step, we'll run a five-year customer analysis. Who's growing? Who's cooling off? Why? It's proactive management."

Bob frowned. "We've just gone off feel. This would be real visibility."

"And then we apply territory intelligence. Assign your sales *hunters* to new business, your sales *farmers* to account expansion. Align skills to opportunities."

Bob leaned back. "We've been assigning based on availability, not ability."

"That changes now. Sales analytics gives you the map. A living, real-time map that shows where to double down or shift."

Bob looked up. "This is the kind of clarity I've needed for years. I just didn't know how to get it."

Jim smiled. "Now you do. And once analytics are in place, we move to the final pillar—**Sales Team Structure.**"

A few weeks later, Jim arrived with a folder labeled "People Plan." Bob was already at the table, coffee in hand, more energized than Jim had seen him in months.

"I've been waiting for this one," Bob said. "We've worked on the what and how. Now it's time to get the who right."

Jim nodded. "Because no system works without the right people in the right roles."

He pulled out a page. " Here is more information from that same study. Here's what we found: *57% had no onboarding process. Only 13% had a documented plan. And just 9% of that group offered consistent training past the first month.*"

Bob winced. "That hits close to home."

"And 91% of companies offer no ongoing training. None."

Jim leaned in. "Team structure isn't just headcount. It's onboarding, coaching, clear roles, training, and alignment with strategy."

Bob nodded. "So where do we start?"

"With a 30-60-90-day ramp-up plan. Training on product, market, and process. Followed by ongoing coaching—every two weeks."

Bob tapped his pen. "And roles?"

"Defined. Hunters find new business. Farmers grow existing accounts. Match talent to tasks."

"We've mismatched people for years."

"Most do. But now we fix it. We'll also set KPIs for each role—leading and lagging indicators. So everyone knows what's expected and how they're measured."

"And coaching?"

"Biweekly 1:1s. Monthly team huddles. These aren't about pressure. They're about support, accountability, and energy."

Bob smiled. "We could use more of that."

"Also, every role needs a clear job description—not just responsibilities, but outcomes. We align the team to the company's mission and goals."

Jim opened his laptop. "And don't forget your sales playbook. It's the manual your team lives by. Talk tracks. Value prop. Objection handling. Case studies. Consistency creates confidence."

Bob nodded. "We've never had that level of clarity."

"That's why we're building it now."

"And marketing?"

"Has to be aligned. One funnel. One message. One rhythm."

Bob leaned back. "We've managed deals. Not relationships."

"Now you'll manage both. And when your team becomes a trusted advisor, adding value to your client interactions — your not just a vendor—you scale not just sales, but loyalty."

A few weeks later, Bob walked into the room different. Calm. Clear. Confident.

Jim noticed it immediately. "You're standing different."

Bob grinned. "We're not guessing anymore. We're building. And the team feels it too."

Jim laid out a summary sheet across the table.

"Let's look at what you've built:

- A Sales Strategy that defines your position and direction.

- A Sales Process that's repeatable and trainable.

- Analytics that inform smart decisions.

- A Team Structure that supports growth and culture."

Jim leaned back. "These are the pillars of scalable growth. Businesses with them don't just grow faster—they're worth more."

Bob raised an eyebrow. "How so?"

"Because buyers and investors value predictability. They want to see you've built a machine—not a one-person miracle. A business with systems scales. A business with systems sells."

Bob exhaled. "Feels like we finally have something real to grow from."

Jim smiled. "That's the point. You've gone from chaos to clarity. From hustle to infrastructure. Now you can lead—with confidence."

Bob extended a hand. "Thanks for helping me build this right."

"You did the hard work," Jim said. "Now let's keep building."

Jim's last words hung in the air as Bob gathered his notes. What they had built together wasn't just theory—it was now an operational reality. But for readers like you, the question might still linger: *Is this model unique to Bob? Or does it scale beyond one company's transformation?*

It does. In fact, companies all over the world have embraced the same core pillars—strategy, process, analytics, and team structure—to create real, lasting change.

Real-World Proof: Two Companies That Did It Too

The following two case studies show how similar transformations led to measurable business success:

Case Study 1: Narellan Pools – Using Data to Drive Market Growth

Narellan Pools, a premium pool builder in Australia, realized they didn't fully understand their customer base or how to focus their marketing efforts. By embracing big data analytics and refining their market strategy, they achieved a staggering 54:1 return on their marketing spend. Their results were driven by clarity on market positioning, improved targeting, and smarter decisions—just like Bob experienced through the Sales Strategy and Analytics pillars.

Case Study 2: B2B Software Company – Sales Structure and Process Rebuild

A mid-sized SaaS company struggled with inefficient sales operations and unclear roles. With the help of a sales advisor, they redesigned their entire sales process, implemented a CRM strategy, and realigned their sales team based on hunter and farmer roles. Over six months, they reduced their sales cycle by 20%, increased leads per rep by 15%, and saw a 30% jump in individual performance. Their transformation echoed the exact path Bob took through Sales Process and Sales Team Structure.

These aren't outliers. They're proof that when a company commits to building its sales infrastructure the right way, the results will follow.

Need Help Building Your Sales Foundation?

If you've read Bob's story and found yourself nodding along, you're not alone. Many business owners and CEOs face the same hurdles—stagnant growth, messy processes, unclear metrics, and sales teams running without direction. But you don't have to fix it alone.

At **Fulkrem Management Group**, we specialize in building scalable sales teams, processes, and execution strategies for high-growth companies. We don't just provide services—we become your trusted partner, committed to driving your business toward long-term success.

Here's how we can help:

- **Stagnant or Declining Sales** – We audit your sales processes and build a turnaround strategy tailored to your business.

- **Lack of Scalable Processes** – We create repeatable, efficient sales systems that grow with you.

- **Unclear Targeting** – We refine your messaging and focus your sales efforts on the highest-value opportunities.

- **Wearing Too Many Hats** – We take the reins on sales strategy and execution, giving you time to lead.

- **Inconsistent Performance** – We bring structure, KPIs, and coaching to align and energize your team.

We understand the pressures you're under. That's why we step in as more than consultants—we become your Sales Leadership Partner. Together we will succeed with your version of what Bob achieved.

***

Author Bio:

Roy De Medeiros has been a driving force behind The Fulkrem Group since 2022, helping business owners design and execute sales structures that create real, scalable growth.

He's worked with companies like Getinge, Cantel, Mad Elevators, and CUTEK Canada to transform inconsistent sales activity into reliable systems that drive revenue—without relying on a single rockstar rep. At Getinge, he led a $60M portfolio across multiple verticals. At Cantel, he restructured national sales operations to improve forecast accuracy and close rates by over 30%. Roy specializes in building repeatable processes that let founders get out of the weeds and lead with clarity, knowing their sales teams are aligned and accountable.

With over 20 years in senior sales leadership, Roy understands the real-world challenges small and mid-sized businesses face—tight margins, shifting markets, and the pressure to do more with less. He's known for quickly identifying where sales are leaking, coaching teams to higher performance, and putting the right tools and dashboards in place so CEOs have visibility and control. Whether it's eliminating pipeline guesswork, shortening sales cycles, or realigning incentives to drive the right behavior, Roy brings the structure and experience to turn your sales function into a predictable growth engine. **Contact us at info@fulkremgroup.com**

Chapter 10

The Power of a Common Goal

Coach Hess

A **Coach's Perspective**

For 14 years, I had the privilege of serving as a head basketball coach, where I learned firsthand the immense power of a common goal. On the court, I discovered how alignment, discipline, and purpose could transform individual players into high-performing teams.

But my journey didn't stop there; over the next three decades, I climbed a steep learning curve in the business

> "It's not about the money. It's about being able to impact and change lives. I took that same winning mentality from the court to the boardroom."
> – Magic Johnson

world—successfully leading individuals from lower or middle management roles to the C-suite. My experience culminated in serving as Chief Advisor for Cloud Services at Halliburton, where I worked at the intersection of innovation, strategy, and global execution.

Through this blend of athletics and executive leadership, I came to appreciate that whether you're running plays on the hardwood or managing multi-million-dollar business operations, the foundational principles of success are the same. Basketball, much like business, is a team endeavor. While individual talent can shine, it's the collective purpose that determines success. A team without a shared vision is merely a group of individuals playing for themselves. The same holds true in business—without alignment, a company will not reach its full potential.

One of the biggest lessons I took from coaching into the business world is that success isn't about having the most skilled individuals. It's about getting everyone to work together toward something bigger than themselves. The moment a team embraces a common goal, it starts to build a culture of accountability, motivation, and performance that leads to extraordinary results. Leadership plays a critical role in setting this vision, but it's the buy-in from every team member that makes the difference. This is how I learned firsthand the immense power of a common goal.

Story 1: Establishing a Common Goal on the Basketball Court

When I walked into the gym for my first season as Coach at Westlake Village High School in Westlake Village, CA, I was immediately struck by the size and talent of my new team. The existing culture of the team had a strong hint of entitlement thinking and the parents of the best players were deeply involved in the program. On paper, we had all the pieces necessary to dominate the game. Scoring wasn't going to be an issue—we had skilled shooters, aggressive ball handlers, and natural playmakers. However, I knew from experience that talent alone wouldn't be enough to create a championship team. We needed something that would unify us, something that would give us an identity beyond just having good players.

I introduced a theme to the program: "Psycho D"—a relentless commitment to defense. Every practice plan included a 30-minute segment dedicated solely to defensive drills. The goal was simple: hold opponents under 50 points per game. This was our common mission, and every player had to embrace it, regardless of their role or personal ambitions. As the season progressed, playing great defense became a source of pride. Players started taking ownership of our defensive identity, and the more we committed to it, the more the wins piled up.

By the end of the season, the results spoke for themselves. Not only did we consistently hold teams below 50 points, but our team chemistry was stronger than ever. Every player understood their role and how it contributed to our success. On the individual level, four players from that program earned full-ride Division 1 scholarships. While talent played a role, it was our commitment to a shared vision that allowed each player to elevate their game and reach their peak potential.

Success in any arena—whether on the court or in the boardroom—requires alignment around a shared purpose. As Magic Johnson once said, *"I took that same winning mentality from the court to the boardroom."* It's this clarity of vision, this commitment to a common goal, that transforms individual talent into a championship team. When everyone understands the mission and sees how their role contributes to it, momentum builds—and remarkable things happen.

During my tenure as Assistant Coach at California Lutheran University in Thousand Oaks, CA, I had the privilege of spending time with Magic Johnson while running his basketball camp. One of the most powerful team-building processes we witnessed that week involved each group being assigned a unique "sound off" chant—used to motivate and unify the team throughout the camp. On the final day, Magic stood at center court and pointed to each group, prompting them to deliver their sound off. To my surprise—and everyone else's—they all merged creating the Michigan State University fight song! It was a spontaneous, unforgettable moment of unity. Individual teams had come together under one shared voice, echoing the spirit of a common goal. That experience reinforced what great leaders already know; when individual contributions align with a collective vision, extraordinary unity and energy follow.

Story 2: The Power of a Common Goal in Business

Years later, as a Business Coach I found myself working with an independent insurance agency led by a husband-and-wife team, Rick and Angela. Their agency was growing rapidly, but with expansion came challenges. Initially, they operated on sheer drive and determination, but as their team grew, it became clear that their success depended on more than just their personal efforts—it relied on getting their employees aligned with a common goal.

Before implementing a common goal, the agency faced constant friction. Employees were focused on individual tasks rather than a shared mission. Recruiting and retaining the right team proved to be a challenge. Sales and operations worked in silos, leading to inefficiencies, miscommunication, and missed growth opportunities. There was frustration at every level—Rick was burning out trying to push sales, while Angela was drowning in administrative bottlenecks. The team lacked cohesion, and the business, though profitable, felt stagnant.

Through communication assessments and business alignment strategies, it became evident that Rick and Angela were a "Super Couple"—each with distinct strengths that, when harnessed correctly, could propel their agency to new heights. Rick was an exceptional sales leader, deeply knowledgeable about the insurance industry, while Angela excelled in systems, processes, and organizational efficiency. However, as they scaled, they realized that success couldn't rest solely on their shoulders. Their employees needed to take ownership of the company's future and success as well.

Angela took the lead in developing a structured approach to performance management. She established a system where every team member had monthly, quarterly, and annual check-in meetings to ensure Key Performance Indicators (KPIs) were being met. More importantly, these KPIs were directly tied to the company's goals and values. To further align the team, they introduced a bonus system tied to the agency's common goal of increasing new business by $2M, ensuring that every employee had both a personal and financial stake in the company's success.

To drive this initiative, Angela identified three key performance indicators that directly contributed to reaching the $2M goal:

1. **New Business Written per Month:** Each sales agent was assigned a monthly quota for new policies, ensuring steady progress toward the annual target. Weekly tracking meetings helped adjust strategies and identify areas where additional support was needed.

2. **Retention and Renewals for Existing Business:** Keeping existing clients engaged was just as crucial as bringing in new ones. The team focused on proactive outreach, policy reviews, and bundling opportunities to maintain a high retention rate and prevent client turnover.

3. **Customer Service Touch Points:** Every client interaction was an opportunity to strengthen relationships and uncover new sales opportunities. The team committed to a set number of proactive touchpoints per client, whether through policy updates, follow-up calls, or personalized check-ins.

By aligning these KPIs with the common goal, every team member—from sales to service—understood how their daily efforts contributed to the agency's success. This structured approach not only fostered accountability but also built a culture where collective wins were celebrated, further reinforcing the momentum needed to surpass their goals.

The impact was transformative. Employees who had previously just 'done their jobs' now had a vested interest in the company's growth. The alignment of individual objectives with the agency's common goal created a culture of accountability, engagement, and high performance. What started as a husband-and-wife operation evolved into a high-functioning business where every team member understood their role in driving success.

Story 3: Turning Goals into a Shared Mission

Another client I worked with had a Survey and Mapping company that had all the right tools—an experienced team, cutting-edge technology, and a growing client base. Yet, despite these advantages, they were falling short of their revenue goals, struggling with miscommunication, and experiencing high employee frustration. The owner had ambitious plans for expansion but had failed to convey a clear roadmap to his team. Without direction, employees focused on their individual tasks without understanding how they contributed to the bigger picture.

The company was experiencing stalled growth, project delays, and inconsistency in client service. Each department operated in isolation—surveyors focused on fieldwork, drafters on map creation, and project managers on client interaction. The disconnect between departments resulted in wasted efforts, redundant tasks, and projects falling behind schedule. Employees were disengaged, feeling as though their hard work wasn't making a meaningful impact.

Recognizing the need for alignment, I helped the owner implement a structured quarterly goal-setting approach. The team came together to establish a common goal for each quarter, ensuring that every employee had a clear role in achieving it. We identified key performance indicators (KPIs) to measure success, focusing on three core areas:

1. **Project Completion Efficiency**: Survey crews and drafting teams were given defined timelines for completing projects, with accountability measures in place to track progress. This streamlined workflows and eliminated inefficiencies, ensuring faster project turnaround times.

2. **Client Retention and Repeat Business**: The company implemented a structured follow-up system to maintain client relationships and drive repeat business. Proactive communication, milestone check-ins, and quality assurance measures significantly improved client satisfaction and loyalty.

3. **Revenue Growth Through New Business Acquisition**: Business development efforts were strategically planned each quarter, with targeted outreach and marketing efforts focused on high-value clients. Each department played a role in the expansion strategy, whether through enhanced service offerings or improved client experiences.

As the company rallied around these measurable targets, something remarkable happened. Employees took ownership of their contributions, knowing their work directly impacted the company's success. Quarterly kickoffs became celebrations of achievements, where milestones were recognized, and top performers were rewarded. The once disjointed team transformed into a cohesive, high-performing unit fueled by momentum and a shared sense of purpose.

By the end of two years, the company had doubled its revenue and profitability, secured long-term contracts, and strengthened its reputation in the industry. With every quarter, they refined their approach, fine-tuning their common goals and continuously improved their processes. What had once been a company plagued by inefficiencies and misalignment had evolved into a thriving organization where success was both a team effort and an individual triumph.

The Bigger Lesson: Alignment Creates Momentum

When teams are aligned around a common goal, something extraordinary happens—synergy takes hold. Employees no longer feel like mere cogs in a machine; they become part of something bigger. Individual strengths begin to complement each other, creativity flourishes, and productivity soars. The sense of accomplishment grows exponentially because each success is shared, celebrated, and understood in context of the company's larger mission.

These three stories illustrate how leadership plays a critical role in setting and reinforcing a shared mission. On the basketball court, the "Psycho D" identity transformed talented individuals into a defensive powerhouse, leading to scholarships and championship-level play. In the insurance agency, alignment on key KPIs and structured performance tracking helped the entire team work toward a collective $2M goal, improving engagement and driving revenue. The Survey and Mapping company overcame its inefficiencies by breaking down silos, implementing clear KPIs per quarter, and celebrating achievements—creating a culture of accountability and ownership.

But these stories are more than just tales of improvement—they are calls to action.

If you're a business owner, executive, or team leader, the time to act is now. Don't wait for the next quarterly slump or team meeting to talk about alignment. Make setting a common goal your top priority. Define what success looks like for your company over the next quarter or year, and break it down into specific, actionable targets. Then, ensure every team member knows how their role connects to the common goal.

Transparency is key. Once your common goal is set, make it visible. Use dashboards, wall posters, digital scoreboards—whatever it takes to keep the goal front and center. When people see progress, they stay motivated. When they see results tied directly to their efforts, they feel empowered. Consistent visual reminders anchor the team in the mission and give purpose to the day-to-day grind.

Then comes the part too many leaders skip: recognition and reward. Celebrate wins—big and small. Launch your quarter with kick-off meetings and wrap it up with success celebrations. Recognize not just the top performers, but those who made the mission happen behind the scenes. This culture of acknowledgment deepens engagement, fosters retention, and builds team morale.

When you get this right, something powerful happens. As team members row in the same direction they begin to gain speed—and not just speed, but energy. Barriers fall. Silos dissolve. Employees start sharing ideas, asking better questions, and taking smart risks to improve processes and outcomes. The team begins to pull, not just for the leader or the company, but for each other.

In this kind of environment, growth becomes inevitable. It's not just about revenue or metrics—it's about creating a workplace where people want to show up, contribute, and thrive. This is how good teams become great. This is how great businesses achieve levels of success they never imagined.

So, ask yourself: What's your team's common goal? Have you made it crystal clear? And what can you do today to bring your people into alignment? Because once you do, momentum becomes your greatest asset—and the results will speak for themselves. —synergy takes hold.

***

Author Bio:

Greg Hess, widely known as "Coach Hess," has spent his life building winning teams, both on the court and in the boardroom. As a former collegiate basketball captain and a 14-year head coach with a 265-78 record, he understands the power of leadership and shared vision.

His transition into business leadership was fueled by the same passion—helping teams align around a common goal to achieve extraordinary success.

A pivotal moment in Coach Hess's life came in 1990 when he embarked on a transformative solo bicycle journey from Jasper, Alberta, to Thousand Oaks, California. This 2,300-mile ride symbolized his drive for personal growth, resilience, and pushing beyond limits—lessons that have become core tenets of his coaching philosophy. The journey reinforced his belief that success is achieved by setting a clear direction, maintaining discipline, and embracing challenges along the way.

After earning his MBA while managing Magic Johnson's basketball camps, Coach Hess spent decades leading teams in various industries, from insurance and oil & gas to consulting and entrepreneurship. A survivor of pancreatic cancer, he has built a leading business coaching firm under the brand of "Coach Hess", using his vast experience in performance management and leadership development to guide businesses toward peak success.

Now based in Houston, TX, Coach Hess has an established track record of empowering individuals and companies to build high-performing teams through structured goal setting and accountability systems. Those looking to accelerate their success can connect with him at Coach@CoachHess.com or text message to 281-744-3341.

Connect with the Authors

All of our Authors love to build relationships. If their chapter resonated with you, feel welcome to reach out.

Connect with the Authors for more information:

Lori Karpman, Lori@LoriKarpman.com

Clay Hicks, Clayton@H7Network.com

Bill Walters, kaznbill216@gmail.com

Donna Grande, Donna@GrandeConnections.com

Jeff Pizzino, Jeff@AuthenticityPR.com

Dan Casanta, Dan@CardinalBusinessFinancing.com

John Kalusniak, jkalusniak@salesxceleration.com

Angel Hicks, InfiniteImpressionsPublishing@gmail.com

Roy De De Medeiros, roy_demedeiros@fulkremgroup.com

Coach Hess, GregHess@ActionCoach.com